THE NEW NOMADS

THE NEW NOMADS

How the migration revolution is transforming our lives for the better

FELIX MARQUARDT

**SIMON &
SCHUSTER**

London · New York · Sydney · Toronto · New Delhi

First published in Great Britain by Simon & Schuster UK Ltd, 2021

Copyright © Felix Marquardt, 2021

The right of Felix Marquardt to be identified as the author of
this work has been asserted in accordance with the
Copyright, Designs and Patents Act, 1988.

1 3 5 7 9 10 8 6 4 2

Simon & Schuster UK Ltd
1st Floor
222 Gray's Inn Road
London WC1X 8HB

www.simonandschuster.co.uk
www.simonandschuster.com.au
www.simonandschuster.co.in

Simon & Schuster Australia, Sydney
Simon & Schuster India, New Delhi

The author and publishers have made all reasonable efforts
to contact copyright-holders for permission, and apologise
for any omissions or errors in the form of credits given.
Corrections may be made to future printings.

A CIP catalogue record for this book
is available from the British Library

Hardback ISBN: 978-1-4711-7737-8
Trade Paperback ISBN: 978-1-4711-XXXX-X
eBook ISBN: 978-1-4711-7739-2

Typeset in Palatino by M Rules
Printed and bound by CPI Group (UK) Ltd, Croydon, CR0 4YY

MIX
Paper from
responsible sources
FSC
www.fsc.org
FSC® C020471

CONTENTS

To Oscar, Haruki and Saga.
Don't ever forget you are a team.

To Aurore, my compass.

'To the migrants from outside who have to cross borders and leave their countries behind at the price of immense tragedies, we must from now on add the migrants from inside who, while remaining in place, are experiencing the drama of seeing themselves left behind by their own countries.'

Bruno Latour, *Où atterrir?*

INTRODUCTION

In the spring of 1864, just as the American Civil War was seeing the launch of a last, desperate, but ultimately successful attempt by the North to preserve the integrity of the Union, a German immigrant named Henry Sieben travelled on foot and by wagon from Illinois to the deepest depths of Montana. From freighting, he switched to cattle and sheep-speculation, and later settled down to build the foundations of two ranches. By the time his two daughters inherited them, Montana had become the 41st state of the Union.

Three subsequent generations have maintained the two farmsteads and expanded them through acquisitions or leases. After a long history as a sheep ranch, the Sieben Live Stock Company is now a cattle ranch. It is managed by Henry Sieben's great-great-grandson Cooper Hibbard, a thoughtful, charismatic and earnest man in his mid-thirties who learned the trade on ranches in Colorado and Mexico, *estancias* in the Argentinian Pampas and cattle stations in Australia's Queensland, and his wife Ashley Wertheimer, the daughter of a Jew from Queens and a North Carolinian of German, English and Irish ancestry.

On 20 December 2016, just over 150 years since its foundation by Henry Sieben, another immigrant to the United States made his way to the depths of Montana. Abdramane 'Abdi' Diabate grew up in Kati, an old colonial garrison outpost in the south of Mali. He had flown in from San Francisco and landed in Bozeman, in the south of Montana, where he was greeted by his college friend Isaac Stafstrom, an American-born Wisconsian of Swedish and Chinese descent. Together, the two journeyed northwards to the Sieben ranch, where Isaac worked on and off as a ranch-hand for Cooper. Isaac had told Cooper about his friend whom he had invited to Montana for Christmas break, and asked if they could lend a hand for a couple of weeks. Cooper and Ashley invited the two to come.

Abdramane's only education until he turned eight had consisted of what he learned on the nine-kilometre trek he took each day with his father, Mamadou. From when Adramane was three, he walked with his father between their home and the family farm in the forest, where they raised millet, sorghum and peanuts in the rainy season, and vegetables in times of aridity. Despite such humble beginnings, he was now studying economics at Stanford University.

It didn't take long for Abdi to realise that the journey to the ranch in Montana from his campus in northern California – a thousand miles away – was in some ways similar to the one he had undertaken when he came to the United States. Stanford University and the Sieben Live Stock Company were almost as foreign to each other as Mali is from the United States.

After a good night's sleep, Abdramane and Isaac gathered with other ranch employees for the first of many morning briefings in the workshop run by Aaron, the ranch mechanic. As they walked in, they were greeted by the sound of American Family Radio, Aaron's broadcaster of choice for news and opinion. This would be the routine every day for the length of Abdi's stay in Montana. Donald Trump's presidency was about to begin. The anchors of American Family Radio were ecstatic. So was Aaron.

Aaron is a dedicated conservative and churchgoing family man. He and his wife home-schooled their three children until they could find places for them in a school specifically approved by their Lutheran congregation. Aaron could certainly get worked up listening to his favourite firebrand talk-show hosts, but he was also a soft-spoken, sweet, gentle man and an attentive listener, deeply committed to helping every Ranch Sieben employee do the best job they could.

The other person Abdramane would interact with the most during his stay at Ranch Sieben was Jeff Seely, who was in charge of 'the Mob' (the ranch's herd of 1,500 mature cattle). Jeff was a veteran of Afghanistan and, like Aaron, a vocal Trump supporter. According to Abdramane, the retired marine was also an adorable, jovial guy, with cheeky tendencies: 'Jeff enjoys a good laugh, and that can include a healthy dose of teasing. He certainly enjoyed teasing me. But it was never mean-spirited. Once I got the swing of his sense of humour, we had a lot of fun messing with each other.'

Abdramane, a Black Muslim whose name means 'servant of the Merciful' in Arabic, an immigrant from a landlocked African state partially overrun by Islamic fundamentalists, was a pretty unlikely sight in Trump-supporting Montana and – on paper, at least – a pretty unwelcome one. Mali, once a sprawling empire but now one of the world's poorest countries, has been the theatre of a protracted conflict since 2012. It doesn't export much these days – smuggled gold in dribs and drabs, certainly; ranchers, not so much.

Aaron and Jeff were sceptical that Abdramane would be of any real help on the ranch when he showed up that first morning, despite their boss Cooper vouching for him. Their reservations had nothing to do with a prejudice against immigrants. Their assumptions came from his education – here was a fancy college kid from California. Cowboying is no walk in the park, in any season. In December, with temperatures plunging below minus 30 degrees Celsius, it isn't for the fainthearted. They gave him a couple of days out in the cold, three tops.

There were initial mishaps, some comical. Up until then, Abdramane had never experienced this kind of bitter cold, but he stoically refused to borrow gear and reinforced boots before they ventured out, having not brought his own. He even turned down an offer of heating pads to put inside his footwear to keep his feet from freezing. He often couldn't feel his hands and feet due to this stubbornness. The retired marine was initially concerned for Abdramane, but was soon poking fun: 'I'll be all right, I'll be all right, no boots,' he kept repeating. The mocking hardly subsided when Abdramane

4

got electrocuted trying to tear live wire with his teeth while working with Polymer, the temporary electric fencing equipment.

In the ensuing three weeks, however, Abdi – as everyone at Ranch Sieben came to call Abdramane – turned out to be very much in his element. He wasn't only familiar with all the basic carpentry tools in Aaron's workshop; he knew his way around the various items used for fencing: the electric tape, insulators and gate handles, the energisers, fencing posts, pounders and connectors. He knew how to latch a hay trailer onto a tractor, how to check the fluids and, crucially, how to drive the thing. His strength and tirelessness, the most valuable currency on a ranch, went a long way in making him universally liked. He would not have achieved this just by sitting around chit-chatting.

Abdramane's journey started when he was three years old. That's when Mamadou began taking him along on his daily treks to work. 'First, we'd cross our little town of Kati and the railway line. Then we'd enter a kind of wilderness and walk for an hour more.' They passed the tiny smallholdings of subsistence farmers and hamlets with populations in the double figures, before reaching their own small farm in the middle of the woods.

Mamadou carried Abdi most of the way at first, but before long they walked side by side. 'These walks were my first experience of the world out there. My dad told me of his travels as a corporal in the French army; where he had been, what he had experienced, and what future he wanted for me.' While on the road, Abdi's father taught

5

him the names of plants and their medicinal properties. He learned which plants cured malaria, those that could calm a cough, and those that were poisonous. Mamadou also taught him what seeds to plant, when to weed them, how to transplant them and the right time to harvest. 'I used to pick a lot of plants on the way to the farm and plant them once I was there. Many of them were mangoes, and now we have a farm full of mango trees I planted as a kid.' His father taught him how to start a fire and use the variety of food crops around them to make a meal. 'He taught me how to read the clouds and how to tell when it was going to rain and how severe the storm might be.' Abdi also learned the names of the different snakes, and what do to if he was ever bitten by one. The district was rife with poisonous serpents and boa constrictors powerful enough to kill a cow. Once, his father was bitten in the head while napping and nearly died.

It's hard to picture the kind of odyssey a daily eighteen-kilometre trek represents for a young boy. Clearly, Mamadou's decision to take his son with him wasn't just about childcare and relieving Nouweizema, Abdi's mum. It was about exercising and learning. Abdi wasn't schooled until the age of eight, but these journeys with his dad made him at home in the world. A decade and a half later, Abdi knew more about economics and America than anyone in Kati, the village where he was born and raised. But like the American ranchers, he also knew about rural life, from harvest yields and weather patterns to the importance of hard work and determination. Those walks with his father as a child were folded into the experience of migration as an adult – he drew on all his resources to adapt to his new situation.

A gifted rider, always eager to help, and always, always wearing a smile on his face – even when experiencing frost-bite – he dug in and went out of his way to get along with everyone. This, probably more than anything else, earned him Jeff and Aaron's respect.

You might have expected Abdi to fear the racism and xenophobia that we are often told is prevalent in places like Montana. But he didn't. Abdi was unfazed on his first morning in Montana and in the ensuing weeks because he had witnessed enough racism in his life, including in Africa between Black people of different ethnic groups and nationalities, to know it wasn't an American or a Montanan speciality, contrary to what many people on his college campus seemed to believe. He also knew, crucially, that xenophobia is primarily a symptom of a fear of the unfa-miliar. We can discuss whether the anxieties behind a fear of immigration – economic fears, political fears – are legiti-mate, but either way, Abdi could tell the fear itself *was* real. He also believed that it didn't make the people who felt it, bad people. What's interesting about Abdi's journey is that it made him acutely aware that while Montanans were cer-tainly more conservative than the students on his campus in California, they weren't nearly as conservative as many people he knew back home: age-old traditions and, most importantly, extreme poverty conspire to keep Mali a far from progressive society.

Slowly but surely, Jeff, Aaron and Abdramane started

getting on and eventually began talking about the elephant – or to be more accurate, the parade of elephants – in the room: Trump, racism, Islam, immigration, *shitholes*.[1] While they disagreed on some issues – mainly the merits of the president – they found common ground on others: love of home and place, deference to elders, the importance of faith in God, humility and hard work. Mutual respect turned into mutual affection and the beginning of a friendship. Montana's flora, fauna and people completely transformed through the seasons of Abdi's stay. When I sent Jeff an email to ask him if we could talk about Abdramane, the answer came within minutes: 'Of course. I miss that Abdi.'

•◆•

Migration often gets a bad rap. And we are fed the news daily that the white working class in rural areas of countries like France, the United Kingdom and the United States of America are against it. On paper, you might expect someone like Jeff to be ill at ease with someone like Abdi. But the two found common ground. They became friends. Abdi brought something to Jeff's community that wasn't there before. The knowledge that he had from his original home was useful in his adopted one. The impact of his presence was not merely economic, it was also cultural. He enriched the lives of those he met, and his own life was enriched in turn.

Migration has become a hot topic across the Western world, and well beyond. Fear and denigration of migrants have fuelled Britain's Brexit crisis, the election of Donald Trump, and the rise of populists and nationalists across the world. The term 'migrant' tends to conjure up images of 'hordes' of refugees fleeing their countries of birth to escape gangs, war, famine or poverty and coming to invade 'ours'.

We think of Syrians and Afghanis on the island of Lesbos, of Africans on sinking vessels on the Mediterranean. We think of caravans in Central America headed for the southern US border. We think of the Jungle in Calais. In other words, when we think of migration, we think of *unwanted* immigration, and we think of it in negative terms. Some of us think 'problem, anomaly, crisis'; others 'curse, ordeal, shame, poor things'.

We've got it all wrong.

Far from an aberration, or something we only undertake under duress, migration is an absolutely central part of the human experience. We don't simply migrate to escape crises, but for all kinds of other reasons besides. The urge to migrate, to quest, to go on a journey, is deep-seated – ancestral, essential and instinctive. If we had no instinct to migrate, the entire human species would still be in Africa. We may even have died out. This instinct led *Homo erectus* and other early humans out of Africa in successive waves some 1.9 million years ago. Our closer ancestors with bigger brains followed a similar path and populated every continent save Antarctica from 70,000 BC onwards. Even leaving out our distant forbears, 98 per cent of our time on earth as anatomically modern humans has been spent as slowly migrating small groups of hunting and gathering nomads. Migration and movement have been the norm, not the exception. Living your whole life in the village, town or city of your birth is a relatively recent, anomalous development.

The vast majority of migration on earth happens without us noticing. Of course, spikes in the speed and size of migratory flows occur due to dramatic events like the wars in Afghanistan, Iraq and Syria and the drought-induced instability and gang violence in Central America. But on the whole, focusing on these crises is misleading. Rather than the brutal, massive influx that fear-mongering politicians and pundits describe, migration is, at its root, an innate human urge. It is overwhelmingly a slow, smooth and quite seamless phenomenon, more *infusion* than *invasion*.[2]

It's not just that we don't get immigration. Focusing overwhelmingly on one side of migration blinds us to the other half of the story – that migration also involves *emigration*. Looking at one without looking at the other is like looking at the act of breathing without considering expiration. It also blinds us to the fact that an emigration revolution is underway. We tend to think of migration as a process by which people from poorer countries move to richer ones.

But for the past few decades, and even in the new era opened by Covid-19, people from everywhere are moving in all directions: from north to south, west to east and, indeed, south to south. There are even 'internal' migrations from village to city (one third of the people who fit the UN's definition of a migrant are Chinese people who have never left the country), and for the migrant these can be as dislocating, or as exciting and liberating, as an intercontinental migration. And many migrants don't stay indefinitely in a single place for ever. Often a migrant moves away, and then moves back. Regardless, the language we use to describe these journeys, depending on whether they are from rich or poor countries, or whether they are young or old, forced or voluntary migrants, can dehumanise migrants and hinder our capacity to see what we have in common.

This book isn't an attempt to idealise migration or migrants. Migration is not the cure to all our ills. When it is experienced as a form of uprooting, it can leave deep scars. Some migrants remain lost, angry or broken, unable to connect with themselves and those who surround them. But let's face it, that is also the case for a growing number of people who don't migrate, and yet feel left behind by globalisation and understandably end up with the most reservations about immigration.

We tend to think of the globalisation debate as a recent one because we coined the term sixty years ago, but it is actually arguably one of humanity's oldest schisms: that between the sedentary fratricidal farmer Cain and his pastural nomad victim Abel; that between those of us who coerced others into staying in place to work the land, and those of us who wanted to keep on hunting and gathering. Framing it this way gives us the opportunity to defuse the moral charge that has been loaded into the migration debate. By looking at our sedentist and our nomadic instincts, we can move beyond simplistic moral explanations for our behaviour and begin to examine its root causes dispassionately.

Concurrently, if migrating is what we have always done, perhaps we could approach it the same way we do, say, ageing? We certainly don't have to enjoy all aspects of the phenomenon (and some of us certainly seem to approach it more serenely than others), but we can agree it's a fact of life. And while there are drawbacks to it, it holds benefits, too. As with life, some of the most precious gifts of migration come only with time.

So what I offer here is an attempt to look at migration from a different perspective: through the lens of emigration, focusing deliberately on positive experiences. It is an exploration of migration's potential as a means of education, empowerment, enlightenment and emancipation in the twenty-first century. I'm going to focus on the people who migrate, within an estimated population of 272 million international migrants worldwide,[3] and zoom in on some of their individual stories. Perhaps, by piecing them together, we can start to tell a bigger story about migration, geographical mobility and nomadism.

Abdramane, whom we met above, is one among many people (aptly described as exceptional[4]) who over centuries have had surprising and incredible adventures traversing the globe. What we will see is that it's not so much that they left because they were exceptional, but rather that they became exceptional as a result of leaving. In this book, we will meet a cross-section of these impressive new nomads who, by embarking on a journey to encounter the Other and discover themselves, are transforming their lives – and the world – one journey at a time. Their stories lead me to argue that migrants and nomads – far from being the problem, perpetrator or victim they are made out to be – are the weavers and the ambassadors of a new ethic that is both locally grounded and globally minded.

Indeed, their stories show that migrating is also about finding a home. Settling down and becoming *of* a place[5] is a fundamental part of the same process. Those who never do get lost in the big picture end up living in a bubble, disconnected from context, culture and the realities of the human condition – a wealthy capitalist I interviewed who flies around the world incessantly was actually annoyed when I asked him what place or places he considered 'home', finding the question altogether pointless, even vulgar.

By first leaving and then settling down, we can connect with both our nomadic and our sedentary instincts and come to see that the divide between nomads and sedentists is an illusion. Leaving allows us to get the bigger picture, to grow personally and to gain a crucial perspective on ourselves, the broader human trajectory and modernity. But to never settle down is to remain stuck with a superficial grasp of the people, the fauna, the flora and all the particulars that make up the culture of a place, to never become an expert of the local, when 'becoming native to a place'[6] is one of life's great endeavours, one of its great gifts, and an important part of becoming decent ancestors.

We will, therefore, also look at the flip side of the coin. Today, all around the world, hostility to migrants, and to migration, seems to be increasing. I mentioned that Abdramane's profile was likely to make him unwelcome in swaths of Montana and the Midwest. I should add that as proud, rifle-carrying, immigration-sceptic Trump supporters, Jeff and Aaron are exactly the kind of Americans that fancy, coffee-sipping progressives from my tribe love to hate. Liberals who rightly abhor the vilification of migrants often end up doing their own sort of vilifying – of those whose views they think they know but don't share, don't understand and see as a threat to their own.

Everywhere in the world, a similar lack of self-awareness is blinding liberals to the fact that their stance on migration is a measure and result of their privilege, rather than a testament to their superior moral fibre. Instead of wearing it like a badge of honour, it might make more sense to start by showing ourselves grateful for it. And to remember that true courage in these times of acute political polarisation lies in the very act of engaging the Other, as Jeff, Aaron and Abdi demonstrated in Montana.

In truth, Jeff and Aaron and other small-town or rural conservatives in the US, Britain and Europe often feel as though migrants and their children are not part of their group, in part because they feel themselves to be an 'out' group, distanced and disdained by metropolitans and their cosmopolitan values. Many liberals like myself who feel well-inclined towards immigrants fail to see that our condescending attitude towards those we see as closed-minded constitutes a form of close-mindedness, too.

These attitudes fuel the far right. Openness to and interest in foreign people and places, if it isn't paralleled by openness to and interest in people who live down the road, is not a virtuous position at all. If a bleeding-heart liberal in London is fascinated by the fabrics worn by recent migrants from, say,

India, but oblivious to or uncaring about the closure of wool manufacturers in Yorkshire, we can understand the disdain that a Yorkshireman may express towards a Londoner's liberal values at the ballot box. And I hope it goes without saying that this way that many liberals think of immigrants – 'Oh, look at their pretty clothes' – while perhaps empathetic, is also condescending. This form of labelling people, of putting people in a box, of understanding them not as individuals but as groups, and groups that are different to 'us', is called 'Othering'.

What is Othering? The term has its roots in nineteenth-century philosophy, with a variety of thinkers using it as a way of indirectly defining where the limits of the self are. Who and what am I? One way of answering that is to say, 'Well, I'm not him, or her, or that.' In the mid-2010s it became a shorthand to describe a variety of forms of marginalisation and exclusion of minorities perceived as a subset or different by the majority[7] (xenophobia, tribalism, racism, nativism, Islamophobia, anti-Semitism, to name a few).

This book is among other things the result of the realisation that moderate conservatives, liberals, all actors of identity politics and even climate activists are just as prone to Othering as those they accuse of it (indeed, as we'll see, we all are). While the chants of 'Jews will not replace us!' heard during the white supremacist rally in Charlottesville in 2017 are obviously a particularly vicious form of this, there are many different, subtler ways that the process can occur. Leave voters have stood accused (often rightly) of Othering immigrants from the EU by Remainers. But Remainers were often prone to Othering Leavers in return. Reducing a Trump supporter to a hat (of the red baseball MAGA variety), a location (rural, Midwestern) and a race (white) is a form of Othering prevalent among liberals worldwide.

Othering is a hallmark of our overwhelmingly sedentary civilisation: the process by which we fabricate and maintain an artificial separation between different parts of a whole; the process by which we assign labels to these parts in an effort to identify and differentiate ourselves from others, us from them, this people from that people, humans from other animals and nature. Othering played an important part in our journey as a species. We would not have developed farms, cities, nation states, multinational companies, without this ability to define and maintain a group. Self-realisation, the scientific revolution and indeed modernity are all premised on it. But it has served its purpose and now become a problem. The time has come to leave it behind.

How?

Just as it has brought the world to a halt, the coronavirus pandemic is an opportunity to pause and take stock of the complexities of our present and the causal link between phenomena – specifically economic growth, energy consumption, (im)mobility, (in)equality, environmental degradation, the rise of religious extremism, nationalism and populism. And to recognise that the prosperity and open-minded, pro-immigration stance of the relatively mobile few is predicated on the relative lack of prosperity and mobility of the many,[8] rather than on moral virtue. The richest 10 per cent of humans on our planet produce 50 per cent of our carbon emissions.[9] It's not too much of a leap to take from this that if we all enjoyed the kind of geographical mobility many people in advanced economies have come to take for granted, we would likely soon be suffocating on the resulting greenhouse gases while cooking ourselves to death.

This points to the greatest, least discussed paradox of the enlightenment narrative: the open-mindedness and progressive ideology it celebrates were founded on violent, unsustainable practices which are still at work today. The pandemic has forced us to stop describing the current crises as deriving from external, exceptional threats to the house of modernity and to acknowledge that they are actually a product of the practices required to build and sustain the house itself.[10]

Most of us are looking for what the Germans call *Heimat*: a mix of home, culture, vernacular, community and, above all, a place where we can make a life for ourselves. And this book is far more about how people feel than the stable metrics we usually use to quantify migration. It is about finding a way to live in the world that supports our desire to leave and our desire to stay at the same time. It is about figuring out how we can be a people on the move, without losing track of where we are. Ultimately, it is about finding our *Heimat*; the place we all long for deep inside. The Hebrew term *Teshuva* (תשובה), which means repentance or salvation, has as its root *shuv*, to turn or return. By extension, it also means 'to come home'.

The title of this book is a tribute to the continuum between migrants, old and new, from our earliest pioneering ancestors who walked out of Africa, to today's young people who are bravely migrating to, away from, and within every continent on the planet. But I am also deeply interested in nomadism as a way of living. Pre-agricultural nomads were both highly mobile and deeply rooted to a place. We have spent the vast majority of our time on earth as nomadic hunters and gatherers, working in small groups of less than one hundred individuals. But the territory each group covered was relatively circumscribed. We made forays outside that perimeter only when we had to. So we were on the move, certainly, but we were experts of the local, too. This wasn't a question of inclination but survival. If we failed to be attuned to our surroundings, we fell prey to predators or the elements. But we didn't – the fact that I'm writing this proves that we didn't.

The hyper-connected jetsetter is a corruption of the original meaning of nomadism. This shallow contemporary understanding of nomadism is misinformed. The word nomad comes from the Greek νομός (nomós), the pasture, and only by extension from νομάς (nomás), the act of wandering on said pasture. We have become so obsessed with the mobility bit that we forgot that nomadism is also fundamentally about place – it is about the pasture on which the nomad wanders, and with which she lives in harmony. It is about local expertise, groundedness, community, family, connection, awareness of limits, frugality. As we will see, the youngest generation is far more in tune with this nomadic duality: a restless urge to travel tempered by a sense of responsibility to do so in a way that is sensitive to the concept of home.

To show how a home is created, to understand what

migration actually is as an experience, and to try to answer the questions that I set out in this introduction, I'll divide this book into two parts. The first part will look at why a person might move, and what benefits emerge for them, their place of origin and their new home. We'll look at this as a series of push and pull factors. We'll also look at the case of refugees. For refugees, it isn't a case of push or pull. There is no choice. And yet a refugee can be just as 'successful' a migrant as any other. Being forced to move is stressful and traumatic. But there is such a thing as post-traumatic growth, as well as post-traumatic stress. That is true for both the individual migrating and the society that receives them.

In the second part, we'll ask what the future of migration might look like in the face of rising xenophobia and a fast-changing world. As climate breakdown continues, there are going to be a lot more migrations. The push and pull factors are going to become pronounced in countries where they currently are not, and many more people will be made into refugees. And yet almost everywhere, borders are closing.

We will end by showing that the various people across parts one and two of this book can be brought together. I believe that returning to the original values of our nomadic ancestors has the potential to solve some of the tensions we've examined. In the future, migration will have to be sensitive to the local, and the frenetic pace of movement over the past few years is neither sustainable nor desirable. Concomitantly, the time has come to recognise the intrinsic violence of the progressive myth, pervasively taught and accepted throughout the world, that a few centuries ago, an elite of brilliant Europeans figured out how to make the world a better place through sheer hard work and ingenuity and that since then, things have been getting better for everyone everywhere, albeit unequally and at different paces. The violence, also, of the meritocratic myth, whether it is called the American Dream, *les valeurs de la République* or something else, and its depiction of a level playing field on which some of us get ahead, while others don't.

Interestingly, leaving our countries of origin allows us to grasp the contradictions in this narrative. As we broaden our geographical and cultural perspective, we gain historical and temporal perspective and slowly come to terms with a civilisation that prides itself on being rational, science-based and pragmatic and yet permits and demands a level of detachment from consequences – made possible only by the ever-increasing complexity of our supply chains – which, as the author and school founder Dougald Hine puts it, used to be the preserve of mad emperors.

Ultimately, what I hope you'll see by the conclusion of this book is both the big picture of migration and some of the many different ways that it's experienced. We can speculate on its future, and marvel at its past and present. Throughout, it's worth remembering, as always, that all of us have a restless, nomadic urge, and that each of us, at some point in our distant ancestral past, is the product of immigration and emigration. People have always moved around the world, and they always will.

Writing in *The City of God*, Augustine of Hippo, arguably the world's most famous North African immigrant to

Europe, defined a nation as 'a multitude of rational beings united by the common objects of their love'. Despite what so-called realists in our body politic and foreign policy establishments have to say about it, becoming a single nation of earthlings united in our love for the planet is no longer a lofty aspiration but a serious pursuit; possibly the most serious and momentous of all. Look at the earth and its creatures as a living organism, a giant metabolism, and use the prism of dysfunctional vs healthy to understand it. Some parts of the organism might be in worse shape than others (indeed they are), but we are all connected.

Viewed this way, perhaps we can start letting go of the contempt and self-righteous indignation which have become the signature political emotions of our age, and recognise that we have a common, mutually beneficial goal. I hope that this book will go some way to encouraging us to feel the pain of the immigrant victim of xenophobia without forgetting that racism itself is a form of unease and disease. Have you ever met a serene, happy white supremacist? Adopting the right mindset allows us to remember that a racist is suffering, too. It allows us to show compassion towards both victims of racism: the immigrant and the racist.

Of course, embarking on an external journey does not guarantee we will embark on the crucial internal journey that may eventually allow us to leave Othering behind. But it can play a decisive role in kickstarting that process.

This is exactly what happened to Abdi and Jeff. Abdramane thrived at Ranch Sieben because his external journeys, from his childhood walks to his international travels, were mirrored by an internal journey that had taught him, fundamentally, that whether you're in Mali or Montana, people have plenty in common with each other.

This resonated with me strongly. Indeed, the peregrinations of the nomads you are about to meet have turned many of them into experts of both external change and inner growth. But, before I can tell you about their travels and the internal journeys they gave way to, I should tell you about my own.

1

THE TRANSFORMATIVE POWER OF MIGRATION

'I have great faith in fools – self-confidence my friends will call it.'

Edgar Allan Poe, *Marginalia*

In Paris on 7 January 2015, two violent thugs meticulously brainwashed by ISIS broke into the offices of the satirical newspaper *Charlie Hebdo* armed with assault weapons and proceeded to methodically execute the vast majority of those present. The attack and the ensuing manhunt left seventeen people dead. Islamic State soon claimed responsibility. The news reverberated almost instantly around France and the world. In what has become a reflexive instinct of the modern Muslim condition, triggered every time abominations are committed in the name of Islam, Muslims in the West, and especially in France, braced themselves for what might come next.

I had developed a keen interest in Arab Islamic cultures since adolescence and eventually converted to Islam when I married a Tunisian woman in 2003. This was required by the law of the land (we got married near Carthage, now a suburb of Tunis, the capital) but it also sat well with my taste for controversy and a naïve desire to stand up for a religion which I felt was being caricatured both by non-Muslims and by Muslims in the West. The marriage was short-lived – we separated in 2005 – but my faith, which was largely theoretical when we married, had become profound by the time of the attack on *Charlie Hebdo*.

One of the leitmotifs of my existence has been an urge to bring together people around ideas. I had become close to a raft of leading Muslim thinkers and politicians in the course of my career, and I turned to them, suggesting that we launch a kind of think tank calling for Islamic reform. Among the Kawaakibi[1] Foundation's cofounders were the former deputy prime minister of Malaysia; the mufti of Tripoli in Lebanon; the late president of the Muslim Judicial Council of South Africa; the current president of the French Islamic Foundation; the rector of the great mosque of Bordeaux; and a Palestinian-Austrian cleric who teaches philosophy at Vienna University, authored a doctoral thesis on atheism and was one of the first Muslim theologians in the world to publicly defend the idea of women becoming imams. We pointed to the dangers of Arabo-centrism – the damaging, disproportionate influence of some of the world's most repressive and retrograde regimes, primarily Saudi Arabia, in defining Islamic norms in a day and age when most Muslims aren't

Arabs.[2] We questioned the wisdom of simply exclaiming 'This has nothing to do with Islam!' in the wake of this and other gruesome attacks by terrorists who thought of themselves as Muslims. ('Would we agree that the Crusades had "nothing to do" with Christianity?!' we exclaimed.) We called for a renovation of Islamic thought and a fresh push for the re-interpretation (*ijtihâd*) of sacred texts to free Muslims from literal, obsolete interpretations.

Converts to Islam are prone to feelings of illegitimacy when comparing themselves to their Muslim-born, and especially their Arab, fellows. As a result, we tend to adopt one of two attitudes. The first, and thankfully the most common, is to become quite reserved. It doesn't look good for the most recent convert to have the loudest voice. In part, that's probably because the second attitude is a sharp left turn towards fundamentalism. I had been a minor pundit and a talking head in the media for years, but as a convert – and to be honest, an attention-seeking missile – willing to be critical of fellow Muslims, I had garnered a significant level of recognition among my co-religionists. A few months later, I woke up to find out that a photo of our launch event had appeared in the latest issue of ISIS's French-language magazine, *Dar Al Islam*. The caption read: 'Conference of apostates.' I was one of the people in the picture. While the text did not contain direct, ad hominem threats, the implication was stark: apostates should be killed.

In the ensuing weeks, France's Counterterrorism Coordination Unit assigned me two elite police officers who followed me around at all times. For about a week, I felt important. Then, the gloom of living in constant fear and the sheer insanity of never, ever being alone kicked in. After a surreal ten months with these guardian angels (I will remain forever grateful for their service and for the French authorities' attentiveness to my well-being), I decided to move to a country in which I knew hardly anyone – and where no one knew me. This was a luxury that the other members of the Kawaakibi Foundation who lived in France, were threatened by fundamentalists far more often than me, and stood at greater risk, did not have.

That's how my two Labradors and I landed in Stockholm in the middle of winter, 2016, where I could move seamlessly thanks to my EU passport (I am Austrian and American). I had never visited Sweden and was drawn there mainly because it was unfamiliar. I was dead broke and jobless, subsisting on cash remittances from a few friends and family for several months. My full-time activity during the previous two years had consisted mainly of not drinking or taking any drugs, one day at a time. I was clean and sober after twenty years of active dependence on pot and a shorter but brutal descent into cocaine addiction. But I had no idea what was going to come next.

The Seattle Freeze is how newcomers describe the difficulty of building and maintaining relationships in that city because of a general lack of interest from locals who can feel cold, standoffish and flaky. When I first heard about it, I immediately thought of my experience landing in Stockholm. Back home, a host of people had – quite understandably – been keeping their distance following my addiction problems, but a few friends remained available and supportive. In Stockholm, no one had a clue who I was (which of course was precisely the point) and, to my utter dismay, no one seemed to care.

My seasonal timing could not have been worse. The social hibernation which grips the country between Christmas and April gave rise to a feeling of isolation and even what I'd describe as a form of social anorexia which I had never experienced before, and haven't since. I had a lot of time to think about the highs and lows, the ins and outs of my life. There had been quite a few. When I got married in Tunisia, the best man had compared me to a chameleon in his speech. This had prompted allusions to Forrest Gump and Woody Allen's character Leonard Zelig, the human chameleon.

I spent my first winter in Stockholm wandering around Djurgården and the majestic city's other islands somewhat aimlessly, re-reading the stories of other, more dramatic real-life characters whose unorthodox trajectories had captured my imagination. I reconnected with everyone from the Russian sociopath Eduard Limonov, whose incredible path from controversial poet in Saint-Germain-des-Prés and New York to ultranationalist dissident in Russia was famously chronicled by the French author Emmanuel Carrère, to Lev Nussimbaum, a Georgian Jew who reinvented himself as the Muslim Kurban Said and became what might most aptly be referred to as one of the great bullshit artists of the 1920s and 1930s. I wondered what life had in store for me.

I've been a tagger and a petty drug dealer; a speechwriter for CEOs of multinationals like Vivendi and l'Oréal; an errand boy for a law firm on Wall Street; a French hip-hop producer and band manager; a web entrepreneur who briefly found himself in close proximity to the world of internet porn; an advisor on media relations and strategy to heads of states, governments and to the then-CEO of French energy giant Total, the late Christophe de Margerie, who became a close friend and mentor; the founder of a movement encouraging French youths to 'Scram!'[3] and embark on a journey to see the world and find themselves. My job titles have included 'Communications Manager' of the *International Herald Tribune (IHT)*,[4] 'President, International' of Cylance, then one of the world's leading cybersecurity companies, and 'surface technician', as the French called my briefly held job as a parking lot cleaner. I have chaperoned a Nobel Peace Prize laureate around Davos and brought a wannabe Indonesian dictator to the Elysée. I have been scolded by Condoleezza Rice for mocking American Exceptionalism in the age of Trump and by my local police chief for smoking joints on the Boulevard Saint-Germain. I have hosted Bill Gates and several heads of states (including some dictators) for dinner. I have also found myself homeless and slept on benches in train stations. And here I was again, unemployed and unemployable.

I can't say that I don't find the effect produced by this somewhat grotesque inventory entertaining. I am well aware that other epithets come to mind, too: reckless, dishonest, entitled and of course self-centred, to name a few. This versatility is itself the stuff of privilege; there is no doubt about that, either. As the effects of drugs and alcohol started to wear off over the years, I was able to see the misguided, decadent, dangerous and immoral aspects of this past for what they were, rather than the exhilarating, glamorous existence of my drug-induced fantasies as an international man of mystery. Coming to the realisation that many things I found exciting and valuable were pointless, that many people who didn't like me much before had excellent reasons to do so and that many others who did like me were just as ill as I was, has been an incredibly enriching process. Learning that not being the self-centred, arrogant jackass I have often been – and could easily become again if I had that first drink or drug – leads to a much happier life is one of the great gifts, indeed miracles, of my existence.

Despite a flawed moral compass and a sometimes staggering cluelessness, with the benefit of a few years sober and clean, I can discern skills and even some virtues that allowed for these baroque situations to emerge, whether they were positive and exciting or grotesque and toxic: eclecticism, resilience, people skills, humour, open-mindedness, a willingness to try new things, the ability to see possibilities and seize on them, to relate to very different people, to clock a room and know what moved people and to connect with them and them with each other. Once I added honesty to the mix and replaced narcissism with self-esteem, I was well on my way to start growing.

These abilities were not the fruit of academic prowess or superior intelligence (despite stellar grades here and there, my overall results as a student were quite mediocre and I ended up dropping out of college). I owe them in no small part to my familial background. I am from a long line of migrants, and they weren't as fortunate as my siblings and me.

•◆•

It is fitting that writing a book entitled *The New Nomads* has turned into the journey of a lifetime. When I first came up with the idea, I had been attending the World Economic Forum, the elitist gathering of business and political leaders in the Swiss alps, in various capacities, for over a decade. Globalism was not just my worldview; it was my identity and my bread and butter. Up until the moment I started writing, this book was going to be a rather predictable globalist ode to mobility. The rise of nativism, nationalism and populism was already a trend. As I saw it, nomadism was the perfect cure: personal and economic growth as the answer to nationalism and xenophobia.

But something started shifting in my mind following the Brexit referendum and the election of Donald Trump. I came to Davos in January 2017 expecting those 'Committed to improving the state of the world'[5] to engage in intense soul-searching and to try to figure out what had gone wrong. After all, it was the Thatcherism-lite of Tony Blair and the centrism of Barack Obama, both celebrated in Davos as the pinnacle of political, economic and social development, which had led to these two earthquakes. I soon realised that there would be no soul-searching in Davos. In the view of those present, in short, the people had 'voted wrongly, against their own interests'. That was that. From climate breakdown to the absurd levels of inequality and populism, the answer of global elites to all our ills remained ... more of the same: more growth, more knowledge, more technology, more innovation (oh, and of course: more mindfulness and yoga classes) would save the day. That's when it hit me: to deal with all these modern fires, our fire brigade is made up of pyromaniacs.

When I started writing this book, I was still a kind of Davos cheerleader and I used the term 'nomad' as many of us do these days: as a shorthand for geographical mobility. When I mentioned the title of the book I was working on during my annual pilgrimage to the Alpine resort, I could immediately sense excitement. Many attendees told me they were nomads themselves, because they 'lived on a plane', owned a loft in SoHo and a chalet in Gstaad, or that their child, a restless spirit, was wandering the world during a gap year. Nor was it only the Davos types who loved the book's title. When I mentioned it to members of the over-whelmingly liberal and climate-conscious Western middle class – London's Remainers, Paris' Bobos, Williamsburg's hipsters – they lit up, too. Mobility and restlessness have become the ultimate status symbols of modernity. The nomad is in vogue. You'd almost forget that not that long ago, nomadism was a dirty word. The nomad was the vagrant, the Gypsy, the wandering Jew, all very unwelcome in most parts just a few decades ago.

I noticed something else. When I'd mention my book to many decent, regular folks with more modest means or from working-class culture, the term elicited blank stares. I realised this difference in reaction to a single word, 'nomad', was an uncannily effective way of knowing on which side of our polarised societies an individual stands.

I slowly became aware of the violence of the aloof, idealised take on migration of many liberals. It was the corollary of what Chris Hedges describes as 'inverted totalitarianism',[6] and Charles Eisenstein as 'totalitarian corporatism'.[7] And it went hand in hand with their aloof, idealised, self-serving take on Humanism, Progress, Enlightenment and on modernity more broadly. I realised that the rise of nativism and anti-migration sentiment is in no small part a reaction to this aloofness.

·•·

The year was 1945. Stalin and Roosevelt knew that a reckoning was coming once the Nazis were defeated. The goal for both was to have conquered as much German territory as possible by the time they met the other camp, to be in a position of power for the negotiations that would inevitably ensue. Breslau, then a medieval German town in the heart of Silesia, now a small Polish city known as Wroclaw, had been buzzing for weeks with rumours of what the Russian troops did to the German civilian populations they encountered as they advanced westwards: looting, torture, rape and murder. Since the end of the Molotov-Ribbentrop pact in 1941, Germany and Russia had been fighting a vicious war that included some of the most gruesome battles of all time. The Americans had only just landed in Europe. Germans instinctively knew they were better off in the hands of the Western allied forces, rather than the Russians.

Late one January night, a group of three women left the town on foot, pushing a cart containing their most valuable belongings. The trio was composed of a tall, breathtakingly beautiful and strong-willed woman in the early stages of pregnancy named Sigrid, her mother Charlotte, known as Mimi, and her grandmother Margarethe. The three women started making their way westwards. After walking for several weeks, they were nearly met by Russian tanks not far from Dresden and had to abandon the cart and hide in a ditch.

Soon after, a truck full of German soldiers heading westwards drove by. Sigrid begged the soldiers to let them ride along. They refused at first, because of the suitcase that the three women still carried. Sigrid did away with this last remaining piece of luggage with a sigh, too, and the soldiers let them on board. In the following weeks and months, they slowly made their way westwards across Germany until they reached the small town of Hof in Bavaria in June. Outside city hall, Sigrid sifted through lists carrying thousands of names of soldiers unaccounted for or wounded, as she had done in every town they stopped in. That's where she saw the name of her husband, Horst.

Horst was no fan of the Nazis; in fact, he hated them. But he was no hero, either. As an engineering student, he had dodged the draft for as long as he possibly could, but by 1943 every last man of fighting age had been conscripted. Still, he had managed to avoid active duty and desk-jockeyed for the German army well into 1944. It wasn't until April 1945 that he was handed a rifle and sent into combat. He was promptly shot in the arm during a pitched battle against the Americans in the forest near the town of Trier.

By the time Sigrid saw his name on the list in Hof, he was in a hospital in Bad Nauheim, a small town quite close to where the Montana rancher Henry Sieben was born. Sigrid grabbed her mother and grandmother, and the three made their way there. By the time the three women arrived and Sigrid was reunited with Horst, she was beginning to have contractions. On 31 August, she gave birth to a son whom they named Alexander – Axel to his family. Sigrid flourished as an actress and was hired in the mid-1950s by Vienna's Burgtheater, the world's oldest German-speaking theatre, where she eventually became tenured and spent her entire career. When she died in 2016, a black flag was hung over the main entrance of the august building.

In the last months of 1968, Axel, by then an assiduous student of law at Vienna University, handed in his application to become a Fulbright scholar. The competition was fierce, and the word among applicants in Vienna was that you should apply for mid-level colleges to ensure you would be selected. Axel thought otherwise, deciding, 'The hell with it. If I'm going to go to America, might as well reach for the stars.' His dream was to spend a year in New York City, one in Paris and one in Moscow before coming back to settle down in Vienna. And so, in the boxes where he was to state his preferences in terms of universities should his application be successful, he wrote:

1. Columbia, 2. Berkeley, 3. Harvard.

As he returned from classes on a warm spring afternoon

in 1969, Axel found a yellow envelope on the doorstep of the apartment, which he hid to spare the family the pain of rejection. Once on his own outside, he took his time before opening it, enjoying the smell and texture of the paper. There was no way that he could ever afford to study in the US without this scholarship. This was his only shot at the American dream.

He got the scholarship. The Fulbright programme would cover Columbia Law School's full tuition costs. He soon received an aeroplane ticket in the mail. On 29 June 1969, he boarded a long-haul carrier for the first time. Destination: JFK. In New York City, he was handed a $25,000 cheque to pay for his tuition fees, which cost approximately half that. The rest was for him to spend on miscellaneous expenses throughout the year.

Alex, as he soon came to be called in the US and from then on, could hardly believe the generosity of his hosts. He could have cashed that cheque and evaporated with the money. Instead, he became a lifelong believer in the American dream and, by proxy, in American exceptionalism – which is precisely what the Fulbright scholarship, one of the most effective tools of American 'soft power' (the active and passive role of cultural influence in international relations) of all time, was all about.

Alex chose to live at New York's International House just off the Columbia campus, with his best friend, another Fulbright scholar from Brazil. The two went out together often and ended up taking two Greek-American sisters on a double date in September of 1970. Alex fell in love with Nikki, the youngest one.

Born in the Bronx and raised in and around New York City, Nikki was herself a pure product of migration. For generations, her family had been moving around. The borders around them moved, too. Her paternal grandmother, Angeliki, was born in a then-Greek port called Smyrna, which is now the Turkish city of Izmir. When Angeliki arrived on Ellis Island in New York on the USS *Berlin*, hailing from Naples in Italy, where she had suffered an amputation after a tetanus infection, her skin colour was described on the manifest as 'dark' ('pale' and 'white' were the other options). Nikki's maternal grandfather Anton, who also made it to the United States, was originally a Hungarian from Sombor, in what was then the Austro-Hungarian Empire and is now Serbia. A gifted horse rider, he joined the army upon arriving in the US and was sent to New Mexico as part of General Pershing's unsuccessful expedition to capture the Mexican revolutionary leader Pancho Villa.

Nikki's Greek-American father, Bill, was born in Albany, New York. He, too, joined the army at a young age and fought on the American side in the Second World War. Alex had at least one uncle who was a known Nazi. Horst and Bill fought on opposite sides of that supreme conflagration of the twentieth century. A generation later, their children married in a small village of the *Waldviertel* during a trip to Austria, a stone's throw from where Hitler's father was born. Life has its ways.

Alex was hired by a New York law firm fresh out of Columbia. After illustrious beginnings as an attorney (in a cherished picture, he stands behind Katherine Graham at a press conference as the owner and publisher of the *Washington Post* successfully fought the Nixon administration's censorship of the Pentagon Papers), the firm asked if he would like to help build their European practice out of Paris. Nikki, who thus far had been employed as a social worker as part of her studies, but also had a keen interest in the arts, loved the idea of moving to the City of Lights. In Paris, she soon became the assistant and close confidante of the widow of Man Ray, the American surrealist visual artist and co-founder of Dadaism. Nikki eventually started her own contemporary art gallery on the Place des Vosges, working with other iconic artists like Dan Flavin, but also less well-known artists in conflict zones from Sarajevo to Kabul. Alex's Moscow plans never fully materialised, though he spent the first ten years of his life in Paris flying to the Soviet capital regularly, which made many people surmise he was some kind of spy.

And that is how my siblings and I, with our Greek, Hungarian, Polish and German roots, and thick layer of Viennese and American culture and values, ended up being born and raised in Paris.

• ◆ •

Most immigrants tend to adopt one of two strategies: blend in or stick out. My mother always preferred the latter. When she moved to France, she built a new identity as a proud Yankee in Paris and Provence. To this day, this is how she is known. She still expresses a cheerful Henry Miller-style disdain for most things American, cannot spend more than a week on US soil without feeling uneasy, and yet is also constantly railing against anything she perceives as European arrogance or xenophobia.

My father prefers to blend in, and only occasionally comes out of the foreigner's closet. He was affected by the unfortunate experience of a distant Francophile family member who had headed to Paris just before the First World War and spent the entire conflict in a French jail merely for being a subject of the Habsburg Empire. In Paris, he immersed himself again, making friends among the chess players of the Jardin du Luxembourg and quickly becoming fluent in French, even absorbing the local slang, though, like many foreign speakers of any language, he curses inexpertly. He has mastered the infinite complexity of French wine, cheese and desserts (in our family, a pastry delicacy became a verb: *to Paris Brest*, the act of eating an entire dish or cake in bite-sized increments over the course of an afternoon or evening, as he loves to do). This endeared him to many French people. Still, the hostile or amused reaction of waiters or cab drivers when my parents, and especially my mother, spoke accented French made it abundantly clear: we were different. To be sure, we were privileged foreigners – despite anti-American and less obvious anti-German attitudes, it's still easier than being African or Chinese. But we were resolutely, unmistakably foreign.

At the same time, day after day, my parents were becoming real Parisians, too, and as is often the case, my siblings Max, Charlotte, Jojo and I played a big part in this. The intensity of friends' dreamy-eyed goodbyes in Vienna or New York as we parted after holidays to head back to 'Pa-ree' certainly weren't lost on me. I could sense that what one dictator once said of Corsica: '*Vogliamo la gabbia senza gli uccelli*' – 'We want the cage without the birds' – certainly applied to Paris and the Parisians, who were quite rude indeed, as far as many people were concerned. Still, Paris was considered one of the world's great capitals. I was proud to be from there. Being a Parisian informed my earliest reading, too – the two authors who got me started were the under-appreciated French giant Marcel Aymé and Enid Blyton. For me, the Famous Five were Claude, François, Mick, Annie and Dagobert: I read every single one of their adventures, but I read them in French.

The limits of cosmopolitanism were also apparent to me from a young age, and many years later, I knew exactly what Edward Said, who taught at my alma mater, meant when he described being 'an uncomfortably anomalous student all through my early years: a Palestinian going to school in Egypt, with an English first name, an American passport and no certain identity at all'.[8]

There were moments when I would have preferred to be from a typically French family like most of the other kids at school. Being scolded by Mademoiselle Demoellon (which, to my and my classmates' utmost delight, phonetically produces *Miss Two Melons*), the dry, severe woman who was my third-grade teacher, for the spelling mistakes of my mother in their correspondence, was a deeply unpleasant experience. At times, I wished we lived elsewhere. Miss Two Melons forbade us from using the restroom outside of recess, and I remember finishing one period, in one of the most shameful moments of my childhood, in a puddle of my own urine, which thankfully wasn't noticed by my classmates. This, and the general tendency of the rigorous French school system to beat you down and see who remains standing at the end of the period, the school year and an entire school career, planted in me the seeds of rebellion; an anger and a self-destructive violence which came gushing out during my adolescence.

I could feel the powerful attraction of blending in, of local roots and sedentarism. For cosmopolitanism to be an asset, you need to be grounded in the particulars (language, people, habits, values, places) of a strong local culture. It can be worthless if it happens in a disconnected void. People who live in expat communities, cut off from those they never stop calling 'the locals', are often prone to the kind of superficiality that turns cosmopolitanism into a charade or, worse, a curse.

I could sense from an early age that complete rootlessness was terrible, and that ceaseless moving around could lead to no more than a superficial understanding of geographies, peoples and cultures. To this day, few things make me as uncomfortable as the bland, eerily detached atmosphere that one finds in the 'co-working' and 'co-living' spaces and the other trendy ghettos of today's expats, themselves rebranded as 'digital or global nomads', that are popping up everywhere. The same goes for restaurant and coffee or clothing chains that look and feel the same in any mall or town high street around the world. A culture which isn't locally grounded is hardly a culture at all.

In the wake of the Brexit referendum, the political scientist David Goodhart offered a handy paradigm to understand

what he saw as the new fundamental divide of British politics.[9] The traditional *haves* vs *have nots* opposition has given
way to a new one, between *anywheres* – self-perceived as
mobile, educated and progressive – and *somewheres* – more
grounded and 'real', conservatives rooted in the place of their
birth. As the son of grounded migrants, I had felt that tension
at play in my life from a very young age.

Thankfully, I was not just an *anywhere* but a *somewhere*,
too. My siblings and I were baptised Catholic (when in
Paris, do as the Romans do) and in catechism classes I spent
a lot of time wondering who these nasty Pharisees were,
whose name so strikingly resembled ours (the *pharisiens*
and *Parisiens*, respectively, in French). Most of my parents'
foreign friends in Paris sent their kids to British, American
or so-called international schools. We young Marquardts
attended French schools, and we unwittingly grew up with
a French worldview. I take this as one of our parents' most
momentous decisions in raising us. I have spent most of my
life describing myself as an Austrian American, which is
what my passports say. But the truth of the matter, as I have
finally come to terms with while writing this book, is that
my elliptic, conceptual thinking, eclectic culture, rather parochial aspiration to universalism and taste for grandiosity
make me French at the core.

The children of my parents' American friends often lived
in a bubble. They didn't follow the references to shows on TV;
they didn't understand jokes and wordplay in French; they
were completely lost and their parents often became quite
panicky as soon as they left the posh 6th, 7th, 8th and 16th

arrondissements. They missed out on much of what Paris has to offer. I felt sorry for them. I am a Parisian through and through – as anyone who has heard me complain in the local vernacular about the weather or traffic on a rainy day can attest. The French countryside and Provence were part of my identity, too: Videlles, the small village just outside Paris where I spent most of my summers until the age of twelve, whose inhabitants called us 'les Amerloques', a one-quarter endearing, three-quarters dismissive way to refer to Americans; and La Croix-Valmer, the Mediterranean village where I spent most of my subsequent summers and where I met the mother of my first son.

My feeling of being firmly rooted in France was enriched, not corrupted, by annual Christmas trips to Austria to visit our grandmother. In time I felt like a local there too. I hated with a passion the itchy Lederhosen shorts my parents forced my brother Max and me to wear in the freezing *Waldviertel*, but I loved sledging down the hill, checking out the neighbour's pigsty and attempting with limited success to milk Mr Sinhuber's cows. Vivid memories of watching my grandmother perform in plays at the Burgtheater and going to hug her backstage cemented my adopted Austrian identity as well as my sense of the weight of history. My grandmother was nine years old when Hitler came to power and, like all German girls her age, she joined the ranks of the *Jungmädelbund* (the younger *Bund Deutscher Mädel*, the female Hitler Youths) the following year. All other youth organisations had been outlawed in the interval. And yet in her last acting role, she played a Holocaust survivor.

America was also a big part of my identity from an early age. During recess at school, when playing war was a favourite activity, pitching 'les Boches' (the Jerries) against 'les Alliés' (the allies), I instinctively kept my Germanic roots on the down-low and overemphasised the American ones. Having a *papouli* ('grandpa' in Greek) who had just retired from the US military encouraged my youthful opportunism. After a distinguished career in the army (he is buried at Arlington National Cemetery in Virginia), Colonel William Economos opened a flower shop in Marble Hill, a minuscule area so far uptown in New York (225th Street) that it appears to be part of the Bronx on the map, although it's technically Manhattan. I vividly recall the water fights my brother Max and I had with the flower sprays in that shop and going to our first Yankees game in the summer of 1983 – I remember distinctly Papou pointing at a smiling old man with protruding ears on the team bench: 'You see that guy? That's Yogi Berra!' – the team's legendary catcher, manager and coach.

Having become seriously rebellious in France and excluded from several schools, it occurred to my by then seriously distraught though not yet completely exasperated parents that it might be the French system that was the problem, and that I might actually flourish in an elite American boarding school, à la *Dead Poets Society*. My father and I visited a few in New England one summer. As an international and therefore benignly exotic student, and one with parents willing and able to pay the hefty tuition fee in full at that, I was offered a place at a surprising number of these schools, despite my already chequered academic career.

It so happened that the most competitive of them, a prep school in Massachusetts called Northfield Mount Hermon (NMH), was also the only one where I came across a number of African Americans and Hispanics during our visit, which made both my father and me happy. There, I met Maajo, an African American from Brooklyn with whom I got into several fights until we became best friends. He and Tamika, his partner at NMH to whom he is now married, taught me about what it felt like to be Black in white America; the subtle racism you were sure to endure – and the risks you took – merely by leaving the city; the nagging, recurring fear of being casually arrested, hurt or killed by police officers. After the brutal murder of George Floyd and the protests that followed, we hopped on Zoom. To them, what was happening in the US was hardly surprising. It was what happened when the institutionalised violence, racism and injustice of slavery and genocide the country was founded upon was multiplied by a factor of Covid-19.

The most momentous travel experience of my youth took place when I was eighteen. Months before finishing high school in 1993, I backpacked all the way to Zagreb in Croatia, just forty kilometres from the front of what was then called the 'war in the former Yugoslavia', with my dear friend Julien. We were hosted by a high-school English professor and were allowed to attend the classes she taught. We befriended some of her students. The boys acted tough, but as we discovered on our last night partying with them, they were terrified of being sent to fight.

This left a lasting impression on me. For the first time in

my life, I was with people my age directly threatened by war and death. I remember being incredibly upset upon returning to Paris and realising that no one around me really cared that a war was taking place at our doorstep. It didn't take long for my indignation to subside, leaving only a sense of shame for my short-lived outrage, a new awareness of the incredible power of inertia. This was my first experience of what the Franco-Czech author Milan Kundera calls 'the unbearable lightness of being' in his eponymous book: repetition in history, instead of teaching us lessons, actually often ends up making us numb to anything, even the most shocking utterances and events.

I should mention one last transformative personal experience. Migration isn't just about geography. It is about social and professional mobility. I had long been drawn to the French hip-hop scene through graffiti, and soon after dropping out of Columbia University in my early twenties, had started coaching and managing a group of rappers. They took the name Apothéose (from the Greek Αποθέωση, Apotheosis, the glorification to divine level) and after quite illustrious beginnings in the underground, were eventually invited to play as the support act of two bands of mythical status in French hip-hop lore.[10]

One night, after a gig at the *Transbordeur*, a small but storied concert hall in Villeurbanne, just outside Lyon, a fight erupted outside. The police arrived and Paps – aka Pacman, the youngest member of Apothéose – was arrested. We spent most of the night negotiating with the cops to have him released, which, thankfully, he eventually was.

We didn't get back to Paris until the early hours of the morning. I just had time to shower before hopping on a train to London to meet a close friend who was dating a young aristocrat. So, a matter of hours after escaping, exhilarated and unscathed from a brawl in one of France's roughest suburbs, I found myself sipping fancy wine over lunch at Apsley House.

This head-spinning change of scenery left its mark. I realised that hanging out only with rappers wouldn't make me happy, just as hanging out only with aristocrats, if that had even been an option, would bore me senseless. I flattered myself into believing that the skills that had allowed me to feel relatively at ease in both environments (though I must say the brawl was less scary than hanging out with the Duke) were innate, forgetting the long tradition of mixing people from different nationalities and worlds that had been the hallmark of the parties my parents threw throughout my childhood. More realistically, I was beginning to sense that migration fostered a versatility and eclecticism which were inherently virtuous. It was because my parents were immigrants that all these worlds had infused in our home. By being in contact with very different people, milieus, religions, musical genres, languages, cuisines, one kept on growing and opening up and flourishing. And indeed, coming and going and bringing different worlds together is one of the great joys of my life.

•◆•

I am a mixture of places and peoples, an expert of sorts in migration not simply through my interests and my professional life, but through first-hand experience. I am neither anywhere nor somewhere, one thing or another. I am both and yet I am far more besides. I am Austrian, American and irremediably French, but I am also the grandson of a German soldier; the great-grandson of Greeks, a Hungarian and a Pole; and the father of a Frenchman, an Australian and a Swede. I am immigrant and emigrant. Through my journey with addiction, I travelled away from myself. Through my recovery, I found something. Something that unites me with Abdi, my grandmother Sigrid, my great-grandmother Angeliki, and with Nikki, Alex and the many others that you'll meet in this book. I found my way home.

2

GOING PLACES

In the spring of 2012, I had an epiphany in a radio studio in Paris. I'd been invited to take part in a discussion on Générations 88.2, the independent radio station where I had first met the members of Apothéose. It broadcasts mostly hip-hop, R&B and Afrobeats but, France being France, airs social and political debates as well. We were programmed to talk about the country's persistently high levels of youth unemployment. Listeners to the station were mostly high school students, delivery drivers, store clerks and other aspiring young people, with and without jobs. The question of the day was: what could kids do to improve their chances of 'succeeding in life'?

The French have a tendency to get hung up on diplomas rather than education. The most prestigious are diplomas from the Grandes Écoles, the equivalent of Oxbridge and Harvard. In April 2019, President Macron called for the abolition of one of the most famous of these, the ENA – or École Nationale d'Administration – in a push to reduce elitism in French society. This came in response to the Gilets Jaunes movement, the wave of grassroots protests which took French elites completely by surprise and brought Paris to a halt in 2018–19, but questioning the legitimacy and future of the Grandes Écoles has been a recurring theme of the national conversation in France, just like abolishing private schools has become one of late in the UK.

This seems like a valid conversation to have, given the inequality these institutions perpetuate. If you're intellectually gifted and lucky enough to earn a diploma from one of them, you're pretty much set. Most French CEOs and politicians are graduates of these highbrow institutions, and alumni who don't end up with prominent roles in politics or the corporate world tend to bend over backwards to find a way of mentioning their pedigree in conversations. Newspaper obituaries often refer to little else (so-and-so was born here, studied at XYZ Grande École and, well, died).

But if you've missed out on this kind of education – or if you haven't performed by the age of sixteen – you're out of luck. My cultural background and privilege meant I could go and study abroad. Most young people don't have that luxury.

In the radio studio, as so often, the conversation got stuck on denouncing the system. Somehow, we couldn't get past the idea that the solution was to get a more diverse set of people to attend these schools. The notion that there might be a problem with the education they provided simply wasn't part of the equation.

There was a palpable sense of frustration and disempowerment during the broadcast. Part of me could understand it, but the negativity was getting my back up. All of us around the table were talking about helping kids overcome the system, but our only answer seemed to be to get more people, and a more diverse set of them, *into* the system. And for everyone else, we made it sound as if their life chances were over before they'd begun. French gerontocracy – government by entitled elders – had succeeded in making us think and talk about young people as if they had terminal cancer. It suddenly occurred to me that there was a form of education, indeed the oldest form of education known to man, which could help empower and enlighten young people in vastly greater numbers.

Thanks to my family's migratory history and my own encounters and experiences, I had become aware that ever-greater numbers of people, not all from rich countries and backgrounds, were crisscrossing the world, making connections, and opening up new possibilities. As the people in the studio argued, my mind drifted to Rachid.

I'd got to know Rachid in the late 1990s when I was running a hip-hop record label in Paris. He was a rapper who had grown up on an unexceptional housing estate in the Parisian suburbs. Rachid was smart, curious and open-minded. I liked him a lot. As a rapper, he performed under the name Ch'klah ('Chocolate') and was quite talented, though he never spent enough time writing and performing to make it a career.

After we both gave up trying to make a living in the music industry, we kept in touch. In the aftermath of 9/11, he lost his job as a baggage handler at Orly Airport – his Arabic-sounding name and a very minor record (he had been caught with hash by the police as a teenager, as had I) were enough for him to be given the boot. Instead of being bitter about this, he turned to art and went back to school to study film while looking for a new job that never came.

Growing up in France as a brown-skinned Muslim can be tough, especially for young men. Rachid was tall and handsome, and his looks left neither women nor men indifferent, whether they realised it or not, but he still couldn't find a job, so he made one for himself. Young hustlers from his *banlieue* had been importing cheap clothes from Thailand for years. This gave him an idea. 'We'll do the 2.0 version,' he told me. With two friends, he set out for Guangzhou in China to buy mobile phone memory cards, portable video game consoles and other electronic items to sell back home on eBay. The three-week trip turned out to be the start of what became a successful, if short-lived, import-export business. More importantly, his brief visit to the far side of the world gave Rachid a new perspective that changed his life – and mine.

French politics and culture in the mid-2000s were awash with anti-globalisation sentiment across the spectrum, from left-wing activists all the way to Jacques Chirac, the conservative president of the Republic. Yet here was a young man from a disadvantaged background – a second-class citizen, effectively – with the courage and wit to look beyond narrow horizons, who had reaped huge, unexpected rewards by going abroad with a pioneering spirit and an open mindset. Something extraordinary happened to Rachid on the streets of Shenzhen, though he couldn't at first quite put his finger on what that was. The transactional nature of his encounters with Cantonese merchants felt surprisingly good. It wasn't that they were warm to foreigners. Rather the opposite, in fact. But their attitudes were a change from the kind of racism that blighted his life at home. One of the Chinese traders called him 'typically French' in broken English.

That's when it hit him. For the first time in his twenty-seven years, *he felt French*. To his interlocutors in Shenzhen, this guy who'd arrived in their midst speaking English like Inspector Clouseau and carrying a French passport obviously *was* French. It never occurred to them to see him as an 'Arab' or a 'darkie', 'Mus' or 'thug', as young French Muslims of North African descent were regularly called in France. To a Chinese ear, his first name was no more alien and exotic than 'Antoine', 'Nicolas' or 'Sébastien'.

At a stroke, in this strange new environment, all the prejudices, suspicions and restrictions that held him back in the land of his birth fell away. What was left was a sense of freedom and limitless possibilities. When he spoke to me about his experiences in China, he seemed to be fizzing, transformed. Rachid had been changed by the mere act of travel and the experience of being seen from a different perspective. He eventually became disillusioned with doing business in China, went on to try his luck in Canada and finished up settling down back home in Paris. But with this foundational trip to Guangzhou, he had opened up to the world, and the world had opened up for him.

Back in the radio studio I finally let rip. I have come to value politeness and restraint of pen and tongue, but they really weren't my forte back then. I found myself shouting to the show's listeners: 'Mais barrez-vous, putain!' ('Just leave, for fuck's sake!') My fellow guests were taken aback, but host Adile Farquane was clearly delighted, so I pressed on: 'The single best thing you can do if you feel stuck is pack your bags and *go*! You're young and dynamic and smart and more adventurous now than you will ever be. Stop talking as if your life is behind you. It isn't! You might think it sucks to be young on the French job market and, in many ways, you're right. But being young and French gives you a massive advantage in the *global* job market. Stop feeling sorry for yourselves! As Europeans, you can do things and go places that bright young Asians, Africans, Middle Easterners, Latinos and even North Americans can only dream of. You aren't condemned to a shit life. Hell, on a global scale, you're among the *lucky* ones.'

Some of the others in the studio were aghast. How could I tell disenfranchised young listeners to 'just' get on a plane? It wasn't that easy. 'I'm not saying it's easy, though it is easier for Europeans than for pretty much everyone else,' I answered, 'but you don't learn much from easy. What it is, is possible. Stop perpetuating the idea that it's reserved for the elite. If people make it from the Philippines, Côte d'Ivoire and Bolivia to Europe, as they do every day, under massive duress, why on earth would you suggest the opposite journey is impossible?' In hindsight, I can see the callousness of that argument. As we'll see, in a world where international mobility has become the ultimate status symbol, there is such a thing as mobility injustice, and there are many people who are never, ever invited to what my former boss Alison Smale[1] liked to call 'the global dinner party'. Pretending that there

53

is a meritocratic way of determining who gets a seat at the table is part of the globalist mythology.

.•.

And yet a driving ambition is a powerful force, especially for young people. This chapter is about the positive pull immigration has for an individual. One journey, physical, can lead to a bigger one, intellectually and personally. In fact, it almost always does. When I was encouraging French youth to leave the country, I wasn't simply talking about the job market and their prospects. The negativity that I sensed in them during the phone-in was the real reason I recommended they leave France. The pioneering spirit that comes from learning how to make it in a different land, the confidence you gain from striking out on your own, even if you fail, is, to me, worth far more than any diploma that Sciences-Po (France's elite political science school) or the University of Oxford can offer.

The common, unspoken thread of education throughout the ages is that it has always been and will always be ultimately about teaching us where we stand in time and space. Education is a means to find our place in the world: in our culture, our society and our age. There is nothing that comes close to travel and migration for instilling a meaningful grasp of this in us.

This immigrant sensibility was epitomised by a young man I met on the Eurostar from London to Paris a couple of years earlier. It was Friday night and the train, packed with tourists and French bankers coming home from the City, was delayed. I found myself chatting in the corridor between two carriages with a guy who clearly wasn't part of either group. Judging from his shiny sneakers, baggy jeans, black hoodie and baseball cap, this guy was from the hood. The French hood. I wondered what had brought him to London. He had to be a professional athlete or a rapper or something. He and I got talking and he told me his story. Like Rachid, Romain was from a Paris *banlieue*. Having tried and failed to get a job with the RATP, the Paris public transport company, he'd heard London needed bus drivers. So he'd shown up and offered his services.

Now he lived in London, driving buses around the city. Like Rachid when he came back from China, Romain was beaming. He wasn't running a major business or starring in movies. But he was the master of his destiny. His English was improving by the day and he was bringing money home to his parents and family on a regular basis. Again, it struck me: simply by trying his luck in a different land, Romain had completely changed his life. There was something deeper going on than finding a job in a more booming economy. By moving around our countries or the world, we change our perspective on things, and on ourselves.

The late theoretical physicist Richard Feynman was one of the most celebrated scientists of his time, but he was also one of science's most original thinkers. Feynman had an incredible talent for *vulgarisation*: the ability to explain very complicated ideas in layman's terms. One of the things he was obsessed with was the nature of knowledge, what the ancient Greeks named epistemology. He liked to emphasise the difference between 'knowing' something and *truly knowing* it. To explain this, he famously talked about how his dad had taught him how to say the word 'bird' in multiple languages, before pointing out that all this knowledge hardly helped one understand what a bird has (feathers and wings) and does (fly, for most of them at least) that makes it a bird.

What Feynman was alluding to was the difference between different qualities of knowledge, from somewhat trivial bits of data to the more coherent sets of information that form culture. The latter is what we expect a solid academic education to teach our children. But the secret wish of every parent is that education will go a step further and make them *wise,* and wisdom is something else still. You might think of it as knowledge that allows us to alter our behaviour; a kind of deep, granular understanding that somehow translates into intelligent, virtuous action. Wisdom comes through experience and the passing of time. It is a dance between the practical and the fantastical that becomes second nature to the accomplished nomad.[2]

Given what we know about the relationship between space and time, i.e. that the two are relative to one another, is it surprising, then, that this special kind of knowledge is itself not solely the product of listening to, reading and discussing ideas? Wisdom comes from the most elementary and elemental form of action of all: that of taking a step, a walk (Nietzsche went as far as warning us against 'any thought not conceived while walking') and, by extension, a journey. An education worthy of the name has always been intimately connected to travel and the increased self-awareness it brings. That's why the diplomas I mention above include a semester abroad as a matter of course. Historically, migrating outside of your comfort zone has been the preserve of the elite. Today, any European from all but the very poorest background can feasibly catch a bus to a foreign country and experience something of the world beyond the horizon. And thankfully, a growing number of young people outside Europe are also able to get the unique taste of where we stand, as a civilisation, in time and space, that this experience allows for.

We have all heard the phrase 'knowledge is power', but for most ancient civilisations, knowledge *was* travel. For the Greeks or the Phoenicians, there literally was no such thing as education without travel, nor travel without education. What made someone educated (and powerful) was the fact that they had travelled. For the Phoenicians and the Greeks, the initiatory journey (Heracles' twelve labours, for example) was a rite of passage, a way of achieving immortality and power *because* of its educational virtues.

The Renaissance saw the practice of sending young aristocrats on journeys to 'fortify their minds' become more commonplace. The travels of the Dutch humanist Erasmus, whose writing breathed life into the very idea of Europe and after whom the European student exchange programme was named, and those of Montaigne and Rabelais, gave way to a kind of rite of passage for young European aristocrats known as the Grand Tour, whereby they toured the continent, usually ending up in Rome, as a means to understand who they were and how to, well, *be*. Indeed, the very notion of Europe, the tapestry of cultures it represents, was woven together first and foremost by travel.

It was around the time of the industrial revolution, when education was democratised, that travel went from being a central feature of education to a side perk. With the first industrial revolution, education ceased to be an elitist project, but it also ceased to be about enlightenment. 'Three Rs' education (Reading, wRiting and aRithmetic) aimed to turn illiterate peasants into competent factory workers. It succeeded in that objective and didn't stop there. Much to the dismay of the factory owners who had introduced it, literacy empowered and emancipated the masses, leading to increased political awareness. But travel had gone out the window.

The legacy is with us today. Most non-elite schools in the world still aren't designed to produce well-rounded creative individuals who have curiosity about the world as a whole and are equipped to flourish in it. Much has improved since the dark days of rote learning, but even now, the education system does a far-from-perfect job of preparing young people for the present, let alone the future. Spending time or living abroad still provides an education in itself. Combined with academic learning it may even have the potential to produce the kind of mass-scale, transformative Enlightenment our age (and the climate and global justice movements which have emerged in the twenty-first century) demands. Our incapacity to change our behaviour in the face of climate breakdown demands a new kind of culture. A culture worthy of the name turns people into grown-ups: we have become a civilisation of unendearing toddlers. What if we allowed travel to reclaim its role as a rite of passage towards adulthood? Then, perhaps, we would learn to act with greater care, as loving parents do in the dimly lit room of their sleeping child.

•◆•

In the examples of Rachid and Romain, we see that we have come full circle. The lessons of the ancients about the pedagogical virtues of travel persist. But today, they are taught to a far greater, broader and more diverse group of people. If your passport or your skin are the wrong colour, travel can still be extraordinarily arduous. But as Abdramane, Rachid and Romain's cases show, it isn't only for the moneyed, and it isn't only for the most gifted and academically competitive, either. Liverpudlian Nicky Allt and Oregonian Jeremiah Caudill have also done their own Grand Tours. And it opened up a world of possibilities for them, too.

School did not get Nicky Allt very far. But travelling to watch his football team most certainly did. Born into a family of migrants from Norway, Italy and Ireland, Nicky grew up in Merseyside in northwest England. It was a tough environment with bleak horizons and little opportunity. There are many words that came to my mind as I listened to him describe his youth when we first talked in the summer of 2018, after I read his memoir, *The Boys from the Mersey: The Story of the Annie Road End Crew, Football's First Clobbered-Up Mob,* and approached him. Privilege isn't one of them. Carrying him through those years was the incredible spirit of community that is embodied by the people of Liverpool, and an overpowering passion for football and his club. Nicky went to great lengths to follow Liverpool FC around Europe in its glorious epoch during the '70s and early '80s, breaking the law, sleeping rough and cheating his way onto trains, ferries and into stadiums.

When I used the word 'hooligan' in our first conversation, Nicky bristled at the idea it could ever have applied to him. 'There never was a racist bone in my body.' My first thought when I heard this was that it rang hollow. In the memoir, there was a toe-curling passage describing how he kicked and stole tickets and passports from a 'typical Belgian' ticket tout before the 1978 European Cup final in London: '... when I say typical, I mean he had the usual pallid skin with that chip-pan black hair. In fact his rug was so fucking greasy it looked like he'd washed it in margarine shampoo. It was slapped on top of a gob that had that anorexic Johan Cruyff look about it. He muttered something back in what I presumed to be Belgian ... '

As Nicky saw it, the passage was intended to be humorous and to catch the voice of his callow, untravelled self, aged seventeen. I wasn't entirely convinced, but one thing was obvious to me: the man I was talking to in 2018 had little to do with the teenager who stole and fought a 'typical Belgian', or anything else recounted in that passage. Nicky Allt went on to build an exceptional career as a playwright. His *Celtic: The Musical*, on the legendary Glasgow football club founded in 1887 to raise funds for poor Irish immigrant families in Scotland, has become a hit, bringing together generations of the club's fans all across the UK and Ireland.

How did this transformation come about? It was travel,

60

of the only kind he ever could or indeed would have considered doing as a kid, following his beloved Reds around the continent, which gave him an education. Nicky probably wouldn't have discovered how much he got out of it, and set in motion the virtuous circle of travel leading to education leading to still more travel, and on and on, if it hadn't been for his original passion for football and just hanging out with the lads. When he eventually started putting pen to paper and became a playwright, some around him poked fun. But many of his real mates, those who had travelled with him, encouraged him. Who knows whether the latent poetic fibre in him would have ever been activated had his horizons not been broadened by football? My impression, and his, is that it played a decisive role.

'I think we [Liverpool fans] were the first to travel away *en masse* because nobody could before the '70s. From the middle of the decade, Liverpool was the best team in Europe and because our team was so good, it got me travelling.'

Nicky's parents were born and raised in Liverpool, but both had immigrant backgrounds – Irish on his mother's side (her maiden name is Fagan), Scandinavian and Italian on his father's (Allt is a Norwegian name). 'I'm a proud mongrel,' he told me. 'Liverpool is a bit of a nomad city, that was always the beauty about it. People in Liverpool wanna see the world. When we were in school, everybody would talk about New York, or Rome, about going to cities around the world. Anybody from Liverpool who goes to New York always comes back and says: "My God that New York, it's got so much like here!" John Lennon, when he went to live in New

York, said, "The thing I love about New York is it feels like ten Liverpools put together." Liverpool never looked inland to England, to Sheffield, to Manchester, to Birmingham, to London. We looked out to sea, to New York, Buenos Aires and India.'

Nicky left school in 1978, at a time when Liverpool's economy was already in decline, 'though not yet decimated by Thatcherism'. He and some mates created 'a little gang' and followed Liverpool FC around. 'We were sort of like football gypsies; we used the football as a passport to travel.' They specialised in 'bunking' (getting on clandestinely) onto boats or trains. One trick was to erase the Belgian destination hand-written on tickets bought from the Transalpino youth travel company and write in a different terminus: Moscow, Rome, Naples, Madrid, Munich or Paris. They would travel without any kind of identification. Listening to Nicky, I caught myself thinking of the Austrian writer Stefan Zweig's depictions of Europe before the First World War, when borders were a rarity in Europe, not to mention passports.

As a child, it was drummed into Nicky that travel was only for rich people, the same way it is represented nowadays. He rebelled against that. 'If you told me, "You can't go there," I'd do my damnedest to get to that place. And we'd get there – I went to every single final.'

Nicky sees the same spirit in immigrants and refugees who are travelling the world now. 'Whether they're fleeing for their lives or just seeking a better life than in their country of origin, they're trying to better themselves. You hear "refugees this" and "immigrant that". But for me, people are just people.' He makes a point of talking to Romanians and Albanians he meets in and around Liverpool: 'The truth is, these kids are us Scousers thirty years ago. We never had money. There was no work. I remember how we were treated when we went to London or southern England. How it made me feel. It wasn't all that different from how these kids must feel.'

•◆•

The first time I met Jeremiah Caudill was in the men's room at Gatwick airport in 2018. Like many nomads, Jeremiah has a knack for making any washroom his own: he was busy shaving, his smartphone in speaker mode playing tunes and him whistling along. I was dressed in a summer suit; he looked like a young Crocodile Dundee. Much less at ease than him, I was having trouble getting the hand dryer to work. I was on my way to Tunisia to make amends to my former in-laws and finally take responsibility for my failed marriage with their daughter. I was surprised when he sprung over to help me out.

There is something uncanny about the maturity and earnestness Jeremiah exudes, still only in his twenties. We started chatting. He was on his way back home to northern California from Sierra Leone. He'd been there for three months, he told me, 'preaching God's gospel'. I thought, *A preacher? This kid can't be much more than twenty years old.* Jeremiah seemed grounded and serene. He felt curious and outgoing. He inspired confidence. All these qualities, I found out much later when we reconnected and eventually

63

met again in Kansas, were not part of the milieu into which he was born.

Jeremiah was born and raised in a cult. He can't recall if it had a proper name. Members called it simply 'the Group'. From his description, it sounds like the Group was half pretty middle-of-the-road American Christian fundamentalism, half 'Patriot' movement, which rests on the so-called county supremacy doctrine that 1) the county sheriff is the highest law enforcement authority, and 2) the United States government has no right to public lands, which should be under local control. His mother, a schoolteacher, escaped the cult and his father when he was six and went into hiding with him and his sister, roaming around Northern California, Nevada and Oregon, depending on where she could find teaching jobs.

Jeremiah was home-schooled, and his memories are of living in the woods in a family full of love, developing a healthy, restless curiosity that drew him to learn things by himself. When Jeremiah turned twelve, his mother Debbie became immobilised by neurofibroma, and from then on was wheelchair-bound. For the next five years they subsisted on welfare payments in a house deep in the wilderness, without electricity, and for two years without even running water. During that period, Jeremiah, his mother and sister lived on $200 a month.

I've occasionally had to live on very little money, but three people living in the US on $200 a month in the twenty-first century sounds pretty grim to me. That's not how Jeremiah sees it. He describes those years as some of the happiest of his life, and when he talks about that time his voice changes. He means it. Their little family was poor but 'emotionally and spiritually rich. We lived in heaven. [Northern California] is all massive trees and pristine lakes, an idyllic setting, trust me.' The nearest town and store were fifteen miles away, downhill, so biking down and back to buy the weekly groceries took hours, and he had to hitch from halfway on the return leg. Jeremiah spent his days roaming the woods on his bike and bathing in swimming holes. 'I fished, shot squirrels with my .22 rifle, helped with house chores, and revelled in just being stupid free.'

At night, Jeremiah would lie down on the floor of the kitchen, spread out volumes of the family's most precious book set, the 2009 *World Book Encyclopaedia,* and read articles about nuclear fission or architecture by gaslight. He was fascinated by technology and history. 'I am not a fan of the cookie-cutter school system,' he tells me. 'I think there is a better way to learn. Thanks to those evenings, I travelled before I travelled. I am grateful I was raised in that mode. I wouldn't trade it for anything.'

When he was sixteen, thanks to his home-schooling association, Jeremiah visited Palau, the western Pacific archipelago best known for adopting the world's first nuclear-free constitution in 1981. The trip was a revelation. It influenced his burgeoning understanding of religion and God. His month on the Pacific islands, living among its people, fauna and flora, introduced him to a peacefulness and a way of life that made him aware of what he calls 'a new conception of the divine. That trip put two sparks in me. One was that I really wanted to have a close connection with God, and the second was that I wanted to see the world and its peoples.'

Over the course of the next few years, Jeremiah 'bummed around' southern California. 'It was awesome. Most of the time, I had no clue what I was going to eat or where I was going to sleep.' The experience changed him for ever. Strangers would offer him a place to stay and a hot meal in exchange for a bit of handiwork. 'Things just kept falling into place. I didn't always get what I wanted, but I always got what I needed.'

He tracked down his father, who was living in Collana, a village without running water three hours north of La Paz, the capital of Bolivia, where, after leaving the cult, he had ended up starting a bakery. Jeremiah began to put aside 20 per cent of whatever he made working as a labourer on construction sites or for removal companies. By the age of twenty-three, he had saved enough to fly to Lima in Peru and, from there, to hop on a bus headed southeast into Bolivia. The town has limited electricity and running water, but his father was thriving. 'It taught me once more that you don't need much material stuff to be happy,' he smiles.

Jeremiah had eventually travelled further southwards and made it all the way to Buenos Aires when he received the fateful call from home. 'I was in Argentina when I learned my mom had been murdered.' Their house had been burgled. She'd had time to call the police, who arrested the thieves, but only after they had shot her dead. A stunned Jeremiah made his own way back. Taking care of all the administrative duties relating to the funeral and the small estate kept him going. As he went through the process of grieving, Jeremiah realised that the single most gratifying thing in life was to give love to others and help them. 'I needed an outlet for that love.'

When he returned to California, Jeremiah asked God in his prayers what he should do next. The answer came, in time. He should go to Africa. Jeremiah had recently seen a movie set in Sierra Leone. He worked odd jobs for almost a year, continuing his practice of setting aside 20 per cent of what he made until he had saved enough to pay for the journey to Freetown. Jeremiah told his church he was going to preach the gospel in West Africa. They liked the idea so much they chipped in with some extra money.

'My trip to Sierra Leone was probably the most impactful three months of my life. Going in, I was pretty nervous. I remember sitting on the plane flying over the Sahara; the in-flight TV displays were only in Arabic or French. I asked God, "What am I doing here?"' It would get worse before it got better. In Freetown, the locals, especially the young, saw him – an American – as essentially a dollar sign on legs. He was constantly asked for money. He kept explaining that although he was American, he was poor. Understandably, this was to no avail.

'For the first time in my life, I experienced what it means to be in the minority, surrounded by prejudice and misunderstanding and your own head that says you don't belong. I was robbed and beaten several times.' To survive in such an environment, he says, 'you need to learn how to forgive, and how to get on with it'.

Once he had found his bearings in the capital, he headed further afield, ending up in Bo, a quiet town, where he planned to catch his breath. No sooner had he arrived than he started receiving invitations from local dignitaries who wanted to charm the 'foreign investor'. He also got invitations from pastors and mission workers who wanted to hear him preach the gospel. Everywhere he went, he was struck by the generosity of his hosts. He would leave even the smallest village with a chicken or a pineapple.

Last time I spoke to Jeremiah, he was in Lebanon, on his way to Bahrain, still preaching the gospel. I couldn't help being patronising, telling him to be considerate, respectful and careful (proselytising is dangerous in the Middle East and, in some countries, punishable by death). I should have known better. He knew exactly where he was and how to behave. In the spring of 2019, Jeremiah announced on social media that he was going back to school. As I congratulated him, I couldn't help thinking that roaming the world had already made him exceptionally self-aware, worldly, grateful and curious by then. Jeremiah, too, is at home in the world.

•◆•

We tend to confine our understanding of learning to what goes on when we open a book or listen to a lesson, but for Rachid, Nicky and Jeremiah, as for Abdi, navigating the world has done a great job of building on academic education or replacing it entirely. Their trajectories point to the incredible virtues of various form of nomadism, from travelling long distances to taking a walk, as a form of experiential education. A small journey – going to see a football match, hitchhiking, walking to the family farm – often leads to a bigger one, opening up their geographic, academic, cultural and mental horizons.

What's remarkable about our age is that the unparalleled pedagogic virtues of migration, especially – though not only – when they go hand in hand with a solid academic education, are better understood by young people across the world than ever before, and more and more of them, though they still represent a minority on a global scale, are able to take part in it. The young people in France I encouraged to head out into the world have long been doing so, and are benefiting in myriad ways. The strongest pull to migrate is to discover. To discover something out there beyond the horizon, and to discover something latent within the traveller. We are a travelling species; we have spread across the globe from a very small patch of land in Africa. Our ability to survive was predicated on our ability to learn quickly, and now, just as then, nothing will cause you to learn quicker than migrating.

The privilege of these 21st-century nomads comes *from* moving, not the other way around. They didn't take off because they were born into wealth. They feel – and are – privileged because they took off. In the past twenty years, they have started to move faster, in much greater numbers, and, as we're about to see, in new directions and with a new and interesting effect. They may not have taken off because they were born into wealth, but, in many cases, taking off can be the prelude to wealth. Why?

3

MIGRATION GOES MULTILATERAL

In a small marketplace in Leeds in 1884, ladies in bonnets and gentlemen in tweed suits browse a small, recently opened penny bazaar. The stall sells everything from collar studs to nails, luggage to yo-yos. When customers ask the price, the proprietor, a handsome, bearded Slav with deep-set eyes and short, cropped hair, points at a sign that reads 'Don't ask the price – it's a penny.'

Michael Marks, a Russian-born, Polish Jew, had come to England from present-day Belarus two years earlier. Like many of his fellow immigrants, he came with little money and spoke barely a word of English. He moved to Leeds shortly after arriving, where he had heard a company called Barran employed Jewish refugees.

He soon struck a deal with the owner of a local warehouse named Isaac Dewhirst to sell his goods in nearby villages and borrowed five pounds to open his first stall at Leeds' Kirkgate Market. His timing couldn't have been better: wages among the working classes were on the rise, and they

70

were beginning to have money for things other than food. The stalls were a hit with the workers and their wives.

The venture was so successful that by 1893 he had been able to open several stalls across Yorkshire and Lancashire. The following year he teamed up with Dewhirst's cashier, a Yorkshireman named Thomas Spencer, to open the first Marks & Spencer (M&S) stall in a covered market in Leeds. Together they opened stores in Manchester, Birmingham, Liverpool, Sheffield, Bristol and Hull. By 1900, Marks & Spencer had expanded to include thirty-six penny bazaars and twelve high-street stores.

In 2009, the company claimed that 21 million people entered a Marks & Spencer store every week. Although it dropped out of the FTSE 100 in 2019, the company still counts 1,519 stores worldwide, employs over 78,000 people, has revenues of £10.2 billion and remains synonymous with British business. Many of the items that Marks sold in his penny bazaars can still be found in the stores today.

Some would say Michael Marks' story represents migration at its best; that it epitomises the positive pulls that happen for a society or an economy when migrants move there. It is so often the case that immigrants are entrepreneurs, go-getters, hustlers. The popular image of people like Michael Marks is bolstered today by immigrant entrepreneurs such as WhatsApp founder Jan Koum, Dietrich Mateschitz (Red Bull) or Rebecca Enonchong (best known for her Twitter handle @AfricaTechie). The stats bear this out. In the United States, immigrants represent '27.5 per cent of the country's entrepreneurs but only 13 per cent of the population'.[1]

There are problematic aspects to the tale of the immigrant entrepreneur our global culture likes to tell, just as there are limits to the hero's journey myth and indeed the American dream as a whole. Michael Marks' story is quite unique. The tendency of our global culture to celebrate the individual and pretend that ingenuity and hard work are the main ingredients of stories such as his goes to the heart of why many people at the bottom of our national and global pyramids are so angry at those at the top. There is, after all, only one Marks and Spencer. But his geographical trajectory is representative of a pattern of migration that endured for two centuries, from the beginning of the nineteenth until the end of the twentieth. During this period, migration was a relatively unilateral business. People moved from south to north, or from east to west, from the so-called developing world to the more developed. There, they did their best to make lives for themselves. Those from Europe who moved south or east did so in the role of colonists.

Through the nineteenth century, England, France, the United States and Germany became prized destinations, followed in the twentieth century by Australia, Canada, New Zealand and Argentina (in 1913, Argentina was the world's tenth wealthiest state *per capita* – largely due to exploitation of the rich land of the Pampas). Migrants flocked to these countries on the promise that if they worked hard, they could create new lives for themselves and their families. During the first great wave of immigration to Australia from 1793 and 1850, when nearly 200,000 free settlers and assisted immigrants from England, Scotland and Ireland chose to migrate there, the country was called 'the land that rode on the sheep's back' for the high quality of life that its natural resources – in this case, livestock – afforded newcomers.

In the United States, the 'American dream' offered political and economic freedoms that many immigrants did not have back home. Some things haven't much changed. In 2018, it was estimated that more than 750 million people would migrate internationally if given the opportunity.[2] And still, Canada, Germany, France, Australia, the UK and the United States (historically and to this day far and away the number one destination) are the top countries people would vote for with their feet.

But an unprecedented shift has occurred over the past few decades. Fuelled by technological advances in everything from communications to logistics, and by growth in trade and less expensive air travel (in monetary, though certainly not in ecological terms), migration is becoming more of a multilateral phenomenon, with more young pioneers moving from everywhere to everywhere and, crucially, back and forth.

•◆•

Moving around the world is generally easier than ever before, though this varies greatly depending on your region of origin, gender, religion, passport and skin colour.[3] Half a century ago, it was something of a daring gambit. If you left Europe for America, there was no easy turning back. Nowadays, if you make a move – which today might be to Shanghai from Dakar or to Indonesia from Georgia – and things go south for some reason, it's far easier to make your way back home. Though it is still very hard for many people to leave their homes in Asia and Africa, multiple countries in the southern hemisphere, which until recently were referred to as 'emerging', have now unmistakably emerged. Between these, so-called South-South migration, especially between neighbouring countries, is increasing at a remarkable pace. This chapter is about the migratory pull that exists at a social and national level – the pull of a strong, exciting economy.

Across the world, in poor countries, but also in richer, stagnating ones, young people are realising that better opportunities may be found abroad than at home. The journey of the New Nomad often starts as a self-improvement enterprise. You could be working in sales in Salvador de Bahia, as a designer in Jakarta, a tech entrepreneur from Poland or Jordan, a gifted hairdresser in Northern Ireland, a talented car mechanic in Angola or simply flipping a mean burger in any small town in America; wherever you are, you may be better off taking your skills to a country where you will be more able to reach your true potential while benefiting the place where you land. In places like Hyderabad, Penang, Maputo, Medellín or Belo Horizonte, where trendy burger joints and hipster hairdressing salons are relatively thin on the ground, you could soon be a successful entrepreneur, running not one but several establishments of your own.

Instead of feeling trapped or blocked at home, more and more young people from everywhere are checking out what the rest of the world has to offer. These pioneers are already key vectors of global integration, and they have extraordinary potential as agents of social, economic and political change. The primary driver of this kind of migration is economic, but we know that once a certain level of buying power and comfort is attained, happiness plateaus.[4] What my conversations with contemporary nomads seem to show is that somewhere around this point, a migrant's external journey gives way to an internal one, and the goal becomes improving their lives on a deeper level, rather than the accumulation of wealth per se. This can take many forms but usually involves connecting with themselves, their community and with nature. In so doing, they become the vectors and creators of a more sustainable, locally grounded, global ethic.

•◆•

Every morning at around eight o'clock, a tall, handsome man leaves his Greenpoint flat in Brooklyn. After a quick stop to grab a flat white and a slice of banana walnut bread, he catches the E train to downtown Manhattan, where his 'nine to nine' job is located. On the way to work, he distractedly checks the previous day's sales of his restaurants and the reports from various managers: sales by category, by salesperson, by store, wastage, food costs, promotions offered. It's all there at his fingertips.

Naveed, who is Pakistani but was born and raised in the UAE, and his wife Aneesa, who is also of Pakistani descent but was born and raised in Milwaukee, both have high-powered jobs in New York City. He is an investment banker at Nomura while she is a cofounder (one of the first employees) of Blueground, a real estate start-up originally

75

founded by Greeks in Dubai. But Aneesa and Naveed also have a business on the side. They are the proud owners of Pizza Pie, a small chain of casual restaurants specialising in deep-dish or Chicago-style pizza. A couple of years after launch, they already have thirty-five employees. But none of them are located in New York. Nor are the restaurants for that matter. The chain is located in Dar es Salaam, Tanzania, and so are most of the employees, though by no means all of them. Pizza Pie has staff in Ukraine, the Philippines and India, too. It takes the world to make good pizza these days.

Countries like China have long been busy flexing their soft-power muscles and rising in global rankings of most-prized destinations for migrants, attracting many people who wouldn't have considered going there in the twentieth century. But another phenomenon, just as remarkable, is that fast-growing mid-sized countries, which not long ago were completely off the radar, are attracting talent and entre-preneurs who aim to cater to their rapidly growing middle classes. Tanzania is just such a place.

Naveed's parents were born in Karachi, Pakistan. His father, one of nine children, was from a modest background, but worked hard in school and managed to qualify as a Chartered Accountant at the age of twenty-one, a rare achievement. He soon got a six-month contract in the United Arab Emirates with Etisalat, a multinational telecom opera-tor, and started his own firm shortly thereafter. Naveed was born and grew up amid the sights and sounds of the never-ending construction site that was Dubai.

As is the case for most migrants, identity was an issue from a young age for Naveed. Being born in the Emirates doesn't give you citizenship. 'The country's extreme oil wealth is shared among the local [Emirati] population, so citizenship is jealously protected, which I can understand,' says Naveed. 'But as a result, there is no middle class. And immigrants and their children who aren't European or American are treated as second or third class.'

Having greatly benefited from it themselves, Naveed's parents had huge faith in the importance of education, and they sacrificed a lot to send him and his siblings to private schools. 'Dubai was part of the British Empire, and you could still feel Britain's influence and worldview in what we were taught, but the students hailed from everywhere: Indonesia, Japan, the Netherlands, the US,' he recalls. This diversity made Naveed aware of a world beyond Dubai. 'That aware- ness changed everything for me. I got a sense that my future lay elsewhere from a young age.'

The chip on Naveed's shoulder, there because he was poorer than the expat kids at his school, stimulated what Naveed sees as a typically Pakistani trait: 'Pakistan is full of entrepreneurs. It is in our blood. Working for someone else is akin to being a servant.' He wanted to feel like a normal kid, so he traded his way up: 'I immediately started hus- tling. It started with sticker books. After that, it was video games. I looked to buy something cheaper from school and sell it in the classifieds, or buy from the classifieds and sell it in school.'

In high school, he applied to universities in the UK and the US and ended up studying business finance at the

University of Southern California in Los Angeles. In the US, to make ends meet, he started trading foreign currency online. This gave him the idea of creating an app for traders: 'In 2009, smartphones were becoming a thing. I had the idea of building an app to deliver news on your iPhone instead of having to go online and sit at a desktop.' This was his first experience of working with people remotely. 'I built the app with an engineer in Pakistan over Skype. We never met. It took us four months.'

The project became his first success: 'I put it in the app store, called it iEconcalc – clearly, marketing wasn't my forte – and it started selling for $1.99. Then I realised it was a very niche app so I could increase the price because big bankers were downloading it. I could tell where downloads were coming from, and the reviews were great. That earned me $500 a month for a couple of years.' But he needed more than that, so he turned to tutoring: 'I tutored people in Beverly Hills, and others in South Central [a notoriously rough part of Los Angeles] – guys covered with tattoos and piercings who wanted to escape their environment. It was an extraordinary school of life.' He had other jobs, too: as a waiter at an Italian restaurant, in a bookstore, and for a tobacco manufacturer.

Naveed graduated just as the 2008 financial crisis hit. 'There were massive layoffs, and nobody was hiring international kids at that time,' he recalls. 'I had one year on an OPT [an employment visa given to graduates] and my only hope to stay in the US was to find an employer who would sponsor me for a longer-term visa.' That didn't materialise. By then, Dubai had grown into a globally recognised brand thanks to the Emirates airline, pharaonic real estate projects and mammoth malls featuring not only shops but absurd activities like indoor skiing (the city's gruesome underbelly of kidnapped princesses and underpaid workers working fourteen-hour shifts in fifty-degree heat was still a well-kept secret). Naveed decided to move back. 'Realistically, that was the only option for me. There was more diversity in Dubai; the jobs were more sophisticated. And I got lucky.' Within six months, he landed a job at Ernst & Young, which would eventually send him back to the US.

In the interval, he met Aneesa on Tinder (which itself was founded by the children of Iranian Jewish immigrants to Los Angeles). She had begun getting a sense of Africa's potential while travelling around the continent on a USAID Public Planning Development project, and then as a tech entrepreneur working around the region for Rocket Internet, a German venture capital firm which had experienced success in building copycat businesses from scratch in emerging markets. By the time the two met, she had some family money to invest and had determined to build a food business in Tanzania. After they had been dating for a while, she mentioned her idea to Naveed, who liked it and offered to help. His experience of building an app remotely came in handy. He designed a logo, sourced the kitchen equipment in China, worked with developers on a customised accounting system, and they set up their first restaurant.

Things did not go smoothly at first. 'Despite decent sales, the business bled money.' Naveed headed to Tanzania to figure out what was going on, and it soon became clear that a

79

few crooked employees were stealing from the tills. He used his *savoir faire* in making things work remotely and turned the small business into a global enterprise of sorts. 'I created a system of controls using remotely operated cameras with guys I found online in the Ukraine and Russia. I got a guy from India to build the Point of Sales system. Through my housekeeper in Dubai, I hired Filipinos to analyse the camera footage from each restaurant to count the number of pizzas made and match that with what is recorded in the Point of Sales system. Meanwhile, on top of the kitchen equipment, I sourced branded balloons, fridge magnets, delivery bags, all that kind of stuff, in China. And I get our branded pizza boxes printed in Nairobi, Kenya, since they have better machines and manufacturing than they do in Dar.'

There are many particularities running a business from a different country: 'You have to interview more people and test them relentlessly. We also have built a level of hierarchies over time that include a junior and senior manager in every branch, along with helpers, and junior and senior chefs in the kitchen. The most important challenge, perhaps, building camaraderie from afar, can be tricky, but Damaris, our Tanzanian general manager, an absolute gem, is an ace at it.'

Besides his daily look at the previous day's results and daily interactions with Damaris, Naveed is on a conference call with all the managers once a month. Aneesa is more focused on strategy. The couple now have three remotely run, locally managed restaurants in Dar es Salaam, and a brand that is getting stronger. 'That's what we are really building. A brand. Our models are Nando's (which is South

African) and Shake Shack.' The two are considering where to go next in Africa. When I ask Naveed how his trajectory as a migrant has influenced the way he runs the business, he pauses to give it some thought and then answers: 'Here I am, I finally made it in the US! But in a way, my real American dream, well . . . it's in Africa!'

Just like Michael Marks of Marks & Spencer, Naveed and Aneesa have turned an entrepreneurial spark into success by applying it to the right geographical context. Naveed, working his many jobs as a young man in the US, was able to sample a whole range of experiences – from tutoring people in South Central LA to making apps. The pull for him was economic success, but I'd go one further and say that there is a self-fulfilling prophecy at the heart of all this. Those who are intrepid enough to move around the world, to be at home in both the UAE and the USA, are those, too, who are likely to start and make a success of a business. The opportunity-seeking spirit that led the couple to open up shop in Tanzania was in play when Naveed first arrived in America as a student and, even further back, when he was at school hawking things from the classifieds as the son of immigrants in the UAE. Migration attracts a certain type of person – the brave, intrepid types with a nose for opportunity and the kind of interpersonal skills to make the most of it. Migration also rewards them. As Naveed and Aneesa demonstrate, with a flexible approach to the concept of home, an entrepreneur can make a business work from anywhere.

•◆•

Naveed and Aneesa are not the only foreigners to have set up shop in Tanzania. Marie Englesson is from Åhus, a small village on Sweden's southeastern coast. Entrepreneurship wasn't a common aspiration in rural Sweden when Marie was growing up. Nor was Africa an obvious destination.

In the nineteenth and early twentieth centuries, religious and social conservatism, as well as population growth and crop failures, led a jaw-dropping 1.3 million Swedes (roughly a quarter of the country's population) to seek a better life in the United States. Most of them ended up in the Midwest, farming or working in industry. In the twenty-first century, Marie Englesson made a similar journey after obtaining a scholarship to study for a year at a college in America's Deep South. She has since spent many years in Africa and experienced plenty of acculturation there, but she remembers Georgia as 'one of the biggest cultural shocks in my life, in a way more significant than anything I encountered in Africa'.

Although the social-democratic fibre of Sweden is heavily counterbalanced by an equally potent brand of individual-ism and capitalism, entrepreneurship wasn't as developed when Marie was growing up, especially outside the big cities, and Marie saw something in the US that spoke to her. Here she was in a small, relatively remote town of the Bible Belt, yet everyone seemed to have a business, if not several. 'The family I stayed with had a small broom company and a little wine shop. I was really impressed. It made me feel like I could start a business, too.' She was also struck by her hosts' generosity and hospitality. 'They were truly adorable, warm people. Swedes tend to be somewhat distant, uninviting.'

Other things she wasn't as keen on. Sweden is deeply secular (Swedes do go to church in droves on occasion, but from what I've seen, it's primarily to sing – Swedes love their singing). In Georgia, everywhere Marie went, the ice-breaker of choice seemed to be something along the lines of 'Which church do you go to?' 'I'm not anti-religious, but in Georgia, having faith means rejecting the theory of evolution. That was already pretty crazy in my book.' But it was something else that threw her off entirely: 'The segregation. People of colour and whites hardly mixed and some people were ostentatiously, almost proudly racist. Even for those who weren't, it was simply unthinkable that I date a Black dude. In 2001!' That settled it for Marie. Her future lay elsewhere.

When I met her in 2016, Marie was running Tanzania's leading cosmetics store chain, which she had single-handedly created and built up from scratch. Her father had left school at thirteen and made his way from errand boy to buyer for a food distribution company. Her mother was a high-school teacher. As a child, her sense of the wider world was influenced more by a friend's grandfather, who'd been a missionary, and by another friend's parents, who were diplomats. By the time she made it to the US, she had already decided she wanted to live abroad, after living in France for six months. Later, a series of internships in India, Malaysia and China convinced her that the developing world was more dynamic than 'stagnant and old' Europe. After university, Marie joined Millicom, a Swedish-owned telecoms company, and spent time in Senegal, Congo and Rwanda, where she found a dynamic, fascinating environment. 'You were easily given free rein to build things from scratch. You were warmly welcomed, as long as you were a builder.'

While many Westerners and Asians see Africa as wartorn and poor, for Marie, this is a typical case of seeing the glass half empty. Without idealising the continent, she felt the vibrancy and resilience of Africa and Africans as a unique asset and developed a deep affection for it. 'From the questions I get when I'm in Europe, you'd think the whole of Africa was either one giant safari park or an ocean of misery and tribal warfare. That's like looking at the US exclusively through the prism of mass shootings,' she says. Marie feels that Africa is hands down the world's most exciting continent: 'I like when things are not structured and perfect. To some extent, it's the chaos that attracts me, for sure. In Africa, I feel alive.'

After a few years roaming around, she spotted a gap in the Tanzanian market that spoke to her feminist fibre. Tanzanian women were still being sold beauty products designed for white skins. 'Playing a modest role in the emancipation of Tanzanian women by offering them makeup that wasn't made for white women,' Marie established herself in Dar es Salaam on her own, in 2011. In 2012 she launched her makeup brand Atsoko ('At the market', derived from the word *sokoni*, meaning 'marketplace' in Swahili). In 2016, Robert Hutchinson, a British-Kenyan veteran of Afghanistan who had just resigned his commission after serving three tours in the Royal Artillery and ending up a major, took a job in Dar. Hutchinson and Marie met that same year, through a friend. The pair soon fell in love. In December 2017, Marie sold Atsoko and moved with Robert to Nairobi to take a break and focus on bringing up the son they were expecting.

What Marie's story shows is that migration itself can turn people into entrepreneurial types. Marie didn't move to Tanzania with a view to starting a business, and she didn't come from a place where entrepreneurialism is celebrated. In Sweden, where corporations are established, and the economy is more regulated and less dynamic, it is harder, as she says, to build something from scratch. There's less room. Whereas in Tanzania, with business infrastructure not as developed, Marie was able to carve her own niche. Moreover, the experiences of leaving the safety and comfort of her place of birth, travelling to the other side of the world, and facing down opprobrium from others based on who she chose to date, before finally settling somewhere where she was a minority, were all character-building. This journey strengthened her independence, resilience and tenacity – key traits for any entrepreneur. Moving from rural Sweden to Dar es Salaam is big, life-altering stuff. When you know that you can handle it, when you know, in fact, that you thrive on that kind of change, starting a business is no big deal.

·•·

One of the last times I spoke with Son Vengetsamy, he switched our audio call to video to show me the view. He was standing on top of a tall building surrounded by the Amazonian forest. The location was Ciudad del Este, Paraguay, at the Brazilian border, where Zulu, his second restaurant in Paraguay, was about to open. The first one opened in 2018 in the capital, Asunción, amid much fanfare. These are not Son's first forays in the restaurant business, but his other establishments are halfway around the world in Dar es Salaam. Son's trajectory is not only a testament to the virtues of geographical mobility as a means of emancipation. It is emblematic of a kind of migration that doesn't make the headlines. Yet it arguably constitutes the fastest-growing migratory trend of our time: South-South migration.

Around the same time Gandhi set sail from Bombay to Durban, South Africa in 1893, Ravendra Vengetsamy's great-grandparents followed the same path and settled in the coastal city where most of Africa's Indians live. His parents desperately wanted a boy and kept having children until they achieved that desire. His father was so happy when he was born, he kept repeating the word 'son'. It stuck. As far back as he can remember, everyone always called him Son.

Son's childhood was blighted. 'It was a tough time in South Africa under apartheid rule, but like in any situation, you adjust. I didn't wake up every morning thinking *This is unfair*. I had no point of reference.' The concept of *shifting baselines* popularised by Daniel Pauly[5] (a term for how the definition of what is considered normal changes with each new generation) comes to mind. Son's pain came from elsewhere. His father was a raging alcoholic who kept moving the family from one place to another in the hope of escaping his troubles, always in vain. 'When it was time to pack up and move again, you never asked him why,' Son remembers. 'You were scared you'd get a beating or be left behind. He loved prostitutes more than us.' One day, when he was thirteen, Son's father told him he would have to open the workshop the next morning. 'I asked: "Why, where will you be going?" He just answered: "I'm not going to be around."' That evening, Son heard the gunshot as his father killed himself.

Son never shone academically and, when he was seventeen, he dropped out of school and started to look for a job. A friend told him that a Spur Steak Ranch, a kind of South African, Native American-themed answer to Toby Carvery or Applebee's, located in a nearby mall, needed waiters. Son borrowed the five rand bus fare from a neighbour and arrived for the interview nine hours early. 'It was my first time in a shopping mall this big and I saw too many white people around, which meant everything was going to be expensive. I couldn't afford even a snack, so I just powered through without having anything to eat.' His patience paid off. The person who interviewed him had noticed him waiting outside all day, and he was hired on the spot for his resolve. He was told to come back the next day wearing black shoes. He didn't have any, so he painted some old ones.

Son worked phenomenally hard and did well in this first job, making over R15,000 (£800) in tips in one month. He was promoted rapidly and accepted a more senior job in another Spur restaurant in the capital Pretoria, seven hours away by car, based on the promise of further promotions, where he worked even harder. Unfortunately, his new boss was terrible. 'All I can say is that he showed me how never to be a boss like him!' One Wednesday afternoon, he received a call from a Lebanese woman called Nadine who also worked for the

Spur chain. She was calling from a place called 'Dar'. She had heard through the grapevine about his tireless dedication and offered him a job in a new Spur restaurant. Son said yes immediately. And then: 'Where is this Dar place?'

The Spur chain's international expansion was not unique. South African franchises like Shoprite, which has long been a household name for many South Africans who buy their weekly groceries at one of its hundreds of outlets across the country, have been expanding all across the continent, one of the motors of the South-South economic development and migration.

That is how Son arrived in Tanzania one evening without even enough money to pay for his visa upon arrival (Nadine had to send someone with the cash before Son was allowed to leave the airport). For his first six months in Dar es Salaam, he worked 14–16 hour shifts every day. He celebrated his first day off with a sandwich – and by sleeping for an entire day. After two years, Son took over running the restaurant. He worked hard at that for a further seven years. It was during that time that he fell in love with Hanna, a tall Swedish beauty whom he'd met in neighbouring Kenya while working for another restaurant there (she was working at UNICEF). He convinced her to move back to Dar with him. Success didn't come easily, but they eventually took over the Karambezi Café, a gourmet restaurant atop a cliff with stunning 180-degree views of the Indian ocean. When I went to meet Son and Hanna, I popped my head into Nadine's office. Now head of operations in the adjacent Sea Cliff Hotel, she still raves about her former protégé: 'You can't make it in the hospitality business if you're not hard-working, but Son is in a league of his own.'

The view came with a hefty rent bill, and for a long time, Hanna and Son struggled. It was a patron of the Spur Steakhouse, a Paraguayan polymath in the telecoms industry named René, who eventually ended up lending them the money needed to get past their tough beginnings ('He was like a good saint to us'). In a few months their turnover had doubled, and continued to grow. Son and René started talking about opening other restaurants elsewhere. Before opting to open the restaurants in Paraguay, the two contemplated starting a restaurant in Myanmar. Further expansion is still in the cards, but it will probably remain in the Southern Hemisphere. 'Many people fantasise about making it in America or Europe. As far as I'm concerned, things are too established there. My added value is in building things from scratch.'

Son is categorical about this: 'I got into the restaurant business because I needed a job, but I never really thought of it as a career. My passion is people. Not so much where they come from – I'm interested in where they're going and in helping them get there. Training immigrants like me and bringing the best out of them. And from my perspective, there is so much more potential, need and, well, appetite in the South,' he adds with a smile.

Son is right. Like Marie, he knows there is so much for people like them who are enterprising, ambitious and ready to roll up their sleeves in the Southern Hemisphere. But while she started in the North, his trajectory is representative of the fast-growing South-South migration that is happening below the radar. This migration is not the kind that economists obsess over, nor the kind which irks voters and brings populists to power in the West. But it represents a crucial lever of development in the countries that have the smallest greenhouse gas emissions (Africa's represent 4–5 per cent of global emissions).

•◆•

Migration is no longer the unilateral movement it long was, but it is still, as it always has been, about the pull of opportunity. With each passing day, more people are moving from what used to be thought of as the global 'core' countries to the periphery, as well as within the core and from one part of the periphery to another. These human migratory flows are being revolutionised and heralding a new chapter in the story of globalisation. Still, regardless of where people are moving from and to, economics is part of the reason. Where people go, money follows. And as we've seen, because of this, migration has an entrepreneurial quality to it. If, when we say 'entrepreneurial', we aren't simply describing 'someone who starts a business', but rather somebody who is enterprising, able to build a network, self-starting, risk-taking and independent, we can see practically *all* migrants as entrepreneurs. Migration is undertaken by those who seem naturally gifted with an entrepreneurial character; furthermore, the experience of migration develops any latent entrepreneurial tendency.

This is good news for everybody, and we would do well to celebrate it accordingly. It takes money, stamina and courage to become a migrant, and those who choose to do so are never the most vulnerable in their countries of origin, which is why foreign aid spent in the hope of deterring emigration has the opposite effect: successful development in almost all formerly poor countries has produced an increase, rather than a decrease, in emigration.[6]

By and large, migrants are also healthier and happier. Couple this with the studies that show, time and again, that entrepreneurs and the self-employed are happier than employees, and the situation can only be viewed as a positive. It's good for the economy, naturally, and that means more money gathered in taxes. It means more jobs. It means new goods. New services. Better education. And all the associated personal benefits that come from having a bit of extra cash in your pocket.

Along with these financial positives comes something that we, as societies, can feel proud of, and, more importantly, united by. Today, the world of business can get a bad write-up from the left, portrayed as bloated, wasteful and impersonal to the point of exploitation. The home of businesspeople has historically been with the political right – smaller state, greater personal liberties, fewer barriers to enterprise. But, today, the right in many Western countries has spent decades developing a narrative of hostility towards migrants, often to cynically shore up support at a grassroots level. A cultural gulf has opened up between left and right that seems ever harder to bridge. Perhaps, though, stories of migration suggest a way to unite polarised nations.

Look at business through the lens of the migrant, and

FELIX MARQUARDT

an optimistic story uniting these two wings emerges. In many of today's migrants, like Marie and Naveed, we see a marriage of two ideals: solidarity with others and the celebration of diversity championed by the left, united to the dynamic, iconoclastic individuality that's lionised by the right. Migrants necessarily cultivate dynamism and creativity – you need to draw on all your resources when you find yourself in a new context where nobody knows you. They are naturally curious and, in the best way, opportunistic: precisely the kind of traits that make them entrepreneurial, and an asset to the societies into which they've moved. But equally, migrants are necessarily aware of the dualism at the heart of identity and identification. Even as a migrant is made aware of how different they are to others, they cannot fail to recognise how we are all the same.

4

THE POWER OF LEAVING

'I must be gone and live, or stay and die.'

Shakespeare, *Romeo and Juliet*

'An unfamiliar city is a fine thing. That's the time and place when you can suppose that all the people you meet are nice. It's dream time.'

Louis-Ferdinand Céline, *Journey to the End of the Night*

Natsuno Shinagawa could be a character from a novel by Haruki Murakami or Mikhail Bulgakov. I could see her following the devil and his cat around Moscow in *The Master and Margarita* or hanging out with Kafka Tamura in *Kafka on the Shore*. Her experience reveals both the joys and complications of migrating from a country that doesn't 'do' migration. At heart, Natsuno is an explorer, a pioneer and a giver. She has adapted to new cultures and places, learned four languages, grown as a person and contributed in countless ways to the lives of the people she has encountered. Though she is only thirty-three, there is something ageless about her energy.

The future of her country depends very much on young Japanese adventurers like her. Singapore's founding father Lee Kuan Yew once said Japan 'is on a stroll into mediocrity' as the ranks of its elderly swell, because of its reluctance to open up to immigrants who could renew the ageing population. Indeed, the future of countries which don't have steady emigration and migration flows is looking bleak. Emigration doesn't happen in a vacuum. It happens hand in hand with people coming in. For countries like Japan, emigration represents an opportunity to open up and renew themselves.

Natsuno comes from a modest background in the Tochigi region, about two hours north of Tokyo by train, a rural area with a mix of the traditional and the quirky in its contemporary culture. It's a very old-school Japanese village, with rolling green hills and rice fields, and 'every once in a while, something like a giant Hello Kitty face cut out in one of the fields. Only in Japan!'

Natsuno's childhood was liberal. With both her parents being teachers, she describes her household as 'full of intellectual effervescence'. She and her two brothers were encouraged to take an interest in serious topics like politics, global warming and animal welfare. 'They taught us to be true to our passions and find a career in something we cared about.'

Twice a year, the family visited her father's hometown in a

remote region north of Kyoto, exposing her to a more traditional Japanese lifestyle. It was there that she came under the
tutelage of her grandmother, a tea master who taught young
women how to behave in society and how to perform tea
ceremonies. As her only granddaughter, Natsuno was made
to sit through hundreds of lessons about traditional Japanese
culture and forced to learn to cook traditional dishes and
help clean the house. 'My grandma was just trying to get
me to be "feminine", but I didn't like the girly stuff. I much
preferred reading books or playing outdoors. That's just
the way they are there. Not much has changed since then,
either. A few years ago, all my relatives held a meeting and
discussed what would happen if I brought home a husband
from Africa. It's not that they're racist. They're good people.
They just haven't travelled outside Japan and have never been
exposed to other cultures.'

Natsuno's parents are far more open-minded, but neither
of them has a passport, nor do they travel within Japan, save
the occasional visit to relatives. Her brothers are similarly
insular. One has never been outside Japan; the other only
left for what she calls 'a typically Japanese honeymoon: three
countries in a week and lots of pictures in front of landmarks.
Box ticking, you know.'

Natsuno felt different. From a young age, she was drawn
to other cultures and the African continent in particular. 'We
would be watching something on TV like *Animal Planet,* and
I'd be fascinated when Africa featured.' As a young girl, she
recalls doing a project on a foreign country. Most of the other
children chose China or Korea; the most daring went with

the USA or a big European country. Natsuno chose Ghana, the only African country she could find a book about in the library.

Natsuno's first experience overseas came thanks to an essay competition when she was thirteen years old. As part of the prize, she was able to travel to Alabama and stay with a host family. She had only started studying English at school a few months earlier, so other than what she had seen in movies, American culture was completely foreign to her. Her host family took her to the movies, to restaurants and, of course, to church. She kept everything from the trip in a box.

'I found it years later,' she recalls. 'It's still a great memory. I kept silly things like a straw from McDonald's, my boarding pass for the plane there, a pen from the church. Like most thirteen-year-olds, I was just beginning to consider what I might want to do with my life. But I already knew I wanted to travel, to see different places and people. I couldn't imagine myself staying in a village like my grandma. I wanted to see the world and learn. I viscerally needed to leave. And I knew the first challenge I faced was mastering English. We Japanese just suck at languages, it's scary. I managed to find a school that had an exchange programme with a school in Australia. My parents could barely afford it, but they sacrificed, and off I went. God bless them! Speaking English has opened so many doors for me. It's the single most important thing I've learned, I think.'

Africa was still the ultimate objective, and after high school she chose to go to Waseda University, a prestigious institution in central Tokyo, because it was one of the few in Japan that offered an exchange programme with Makerere University in Kampala, the capital of Uganda. Natsuno became Makerere's first Japanese student to enrol for a full year. The experience didn't live up to her expectations ('despite a prestigious past, that uni was just too dysfunctional and political in the ugly sense of the word') but during school break she decided to go hitchhiking across Tanzania, Malawi and Mozambique, and that was an absolute revelation. Not that it was all fun. While in Mozambique, she contracted malaria and was admitted into a hospital in Maputo for ten days. 'That was actually one of the worst experiences of my life.' But she had felt the thrill of travelling and found university life frustrating in comparison when she returned. She also realised that she had learned much more travelling on foot and hitching rides than she had sitting in class.

Before her trip, Natsuno had organised some internships to do during her summer break in order to improve her job prospects. But she decided that going travelling again would not only be more exciting, it would be better for her future. She spent the next four months on the move from the Equator to Egypt, stopping in Tanzania, Kenya, Ethiopia and Sudan.

When Natsuno returned to Japan, she soon found something was terribly off in the life waiting for her there. All her friends were looking for jobs. They had all been free together as students, but now the party was over and they were all preparing to enter the rat race. She couldn't stand it. A friend in France worked for a company that helped Africans in Europe connect with their families in French-speaking Africa. This provided a wonderful excuse to escape Japan. She started learning French in Côte d'Ivoire, which is a bit like learning English in Jamaica. People she met when she first tried out her French in France understood what she was saying, but couldn't process the fact that a petite Japanese woman would speak with an Ivorian accent. Natsuno sounds like what my friends from French-speaking Africa would call une blédarde, from the Arabic *bled* (بلد), the village: an African from back home.

Back in Tokyo, she finished her degree in Development Arts and took courses to 'normalise' her French. This led to her work as a translator and fixer for French journalists covering the Fukushima earthquake and its aftermath. There were also trips to Iran and Algeria. But Natsuno could not see a future for herself in Japan. She knew the social pressure of being considered a bad apple in her patriarchal home country, especially as a young woman, but it was the first time she really experienced it. A major identity crisis ensued. Natsuno knew she wouldn't flourish in the country of her birth, and that the freedom of being able to choose what she wanted to do and where she wanted to be was one of the things she held most dear. But this desire conflicted with her culture and society. The crisis lasted almost three years.

Her break came. She heard of a job opening at the Japanese embassy in Senegal, working with local NGOs. 'I knew this was it. I never looked back.' After two years that she describes as 'possibly the happiest in my life', she left the embassy for a succession of jobs all around Africa, from Mali to South Sudan. Early in 2018, she was hired to work on the Anzisha Prize, which goes to talented and resourceful young entrepreneurs from across the continent. Natsuno is passionate about job creation in communities affected by war and conflict, so this suits her perfectly. Part of her always wanted to be a writer, to build something, or create something, 'but for now, I'm fully dedicated to Anzisha'.

•◆•

As I was researching this book, the same thing kept occurring. Having heard that I was writing about migration, people would take it for granted that it was essentially about immigration. Whether we look on migration favourably, with scepticism or outright hostility, we tend to focus on people coming into 'our' countries and ignore the other half of the phenomenon. People tend to disconnect immigration and emigration so much that a poll taken in Britain in the months leading up to the EU referendum found that a majority of Britons somehow felt they should be free to work and live in the EU, but that EU citizens should not be free to do so in Britain.

But, as I said earlier, looking at immigration without looking at emigration is like considering the act of breathing without taking into account expiration. Keeping in mind that migration is a natural urge and part of the same process as immigration allows us to see the latter as natural, too, not the invasion described by the Trump administration, which regularly referred to immigrants as 'foreign invaders' responsible for serious infectious diseases, drug running, gang violence, human trafficking and terrorism.

Emigration is often also about the transformative power of leaving one's home behind, as it was for Natsuno. Among the reasons that people decide to join the ranks of the new nomads is that migration can give them the opportunity to be who they really want to be and to do what they want to do, without the pressures they face from familial or societal expectations at home.

Our personal and national identities, our families, backgrounds, educations, careers and relationships – all these things give meaning to our lives. But they can also be stifling. There isn't the slightest doubt in my mind that my father's urge to get away from Germany had a lot to do with the weight of the country's Nazi past (it also likely explains why the majority of his closest friends are Jewish). Nor is there any doubt in my mind that the specific brand of British Euroscepticism which eventually produced Brexit is intimately linked to the nostalgic, imperial vision of Britain contained in the school manuals of Boris Johnson, as academics Danny Dorling and Sally Tomlinson have compellingly argued.[1]

It's a Britain that exists in the time just after a sort of parallel universe Second World War, with Britain the uncomplicated heroic victor, home of the Spitfire, Keep Calm and Carry On sangfroid, and bunting hung up in every street. It is a vision of that conflict that studiously ignores, for example, British culpability for the Bengal famine of 1943. Perhaps Britain is the wrong word – this is a particularly English phenomenon.

Nevertheless, this stifling atmosphere may be why, since the Brexit vote, a study by academics at the University of Oxford and the Berlin Social Science Centre found that emigration from Britain to the EU was, by October 2019, at a ten-year high. An estimated 84,000 UK citizens migrated to the EU in 2019, up from 58,000 the year before the Brexit vote in 2015, and 46,000 back in 2012.[2] A study by the OECD and Eurostat in 2020 showed that there was a 500 per cent increase in those who had made a move to, and then took up citizenship in, an EU state. Germany, for instance, saw a 2,000 per cent rise in Britons naturalising there. The principal reason cited was the loss of freedom of movement that the new, post-Brexit, British passport conveys. Daniel Tetlow, the study's co-author, commented that this rise in naturalisation numbers showed a striking commitment 'to integrate or socially embed'. These are Britons who are leaving Britain behind.[3]

Others chase an image of happiness implanted in them in early childhood, only to find at some point that what they've been pursuing doesn't quite fit, that they want something else. Many of the nomads I spoke to have gone through this kind of identity crisis prior to migrating. They realised that they were unhappy with their lives, but felt trapped in their context. They had jobs and relationships and obligations, all of which meant they were expected to carry on as though nothing had changed. But they weren't the same – something fundamental had altered.

•◆•

While some, like Natsuno, have a feeling from a young age that they will be smothered if they don't leave, others like Jamie Sanbar realise it almost overnight. Jamie, a young Australian who now lives in London, thought that he could live out his life comfortably in a traditional Muslim family. But when he finally came to terms with his sexual preferences, the conservative lifestyle of his family prevented him from coming out. It was only by leaving Australia behind that Jamie was able to live his life freely as a gay man.

Like many second-generation Australians in Sydney's inner-western suburbs, Jamie often felt he was stuck between two conflicting worlds. On the one side was the traditional Muslim world that his parents inhabited; on the other, the liberal values that urban Australia promoted. 'It never felt like I fit in with either side. I was too Lebanese for the whites and too white for the Lebanese.'

Jamie's father grew up in Beirut. As one of the older boys of the family, he had to leave school at a young age to sell candy and tobacco on the street in order to support the family. He arrived in Sydney in his early twenties, seeking refuge from the Lebanese civil war without knowing a word of English. Jamie's mother is the daughter of Russians who had fled their country in the aftermath of the 1917 Bolshevik revolution. Her own mother grew up in Harbin, a city in northern China which became a hub for White Russian émigrés, before ending up in Hobart in Australia, where some Russians had offered to sponsor her.

Jamie's parents met in a fruit shop in Sydney. They fell in love and started a backyard paving business. Like many migrants from Lebanon's poor south, Jamie's father could neither read nor write. But his years as a street vendor had turned him into a gifted tradesman and taught him how to gain people's confidence. Jamie's mother, meanwhile, was cool and systematic and ran the administrative side of the business, which began to take off. What started off as a chatty Lebanese guy and his girlfriend driving around in a rundown red truck quickly became a small empire. Their timing was great: the construction industry in Sydney was just beginning to boom. 'At the same time, they were grafters. My father would often sleep in his car on construction sites. My mum used to take us to visit him on weekends and even then he'd make us work alongside the boys laying the pavers.'

His parents' success meant that Jamie grew up with all the accoutrements of privilege. The family home in Strathfield was lavish, complete with tennis court and swimming pool. Jamie and his siblings were sent to the best private schools in the area and then to top universities. On the surface, the family seemed to have smoothly integrated into Australian life. To neighbours and friends, they were the archetypal Australian success story. But cultural tensions were smouldering under the surface.

Jamie's father was 'about as Aussie as they come nowadays'. But along with his strong Aussie accent came very traditional views on family life, rooted in his upbringing. 'In his mind, we're all meant to stay at home until we're married and work for the family business.' That was the world Jamie's father came from and knew – you survive by sticking together. It is a striking irony that Jamie's father, a migrant, was somebody who wanted to tie his son down to a place, and a way of life. As he saw it, he had worked his entire life so that his family didn't need to struggle the way he did. 'Wanting to do anything else was throwing all that hard work back in his face,' Jamie reflects.

Jamie studied literature against his parents' wishes, his way of saying he didn't want the life they envisaged for him. He tried getting a job as a journalist upon graduating but knew no one in the business and got nowhere. He gave that up and got 'a real job', as his brother and father saw it, in the mining business. Three years later, he had risen to oversee large-scale commercial public works projects. 'For a while, it felt right. I'd finally proven myself. For a lot of my early life, at school and then at university, I felt useless.'

Then, in December 2014, one of Jamie's close colleagues died suddenly of a brain aneurysm. 'I remember her coming into my office to say goodbye. She was off to buy her niece a Christmas present. A couple of hours later, I got the call that she had collapsed and was in hospital. By the time I arrived, she had died.' The experience had a profound impact on Jamie's mental health. He became highly anxious and began to have panic attacks. 'I couldn't eat or sleep. I was trauma-tised. At first, I thought it was the shock of it all – somebody so close dying so suddenly. But even after the funeral when things started to normalise again, I never felt quite like myself.' Becoming aware of his own mortality made Jamie realise how unsatisfied with his life he really was. 'I had been fooling myself for years, telling myself that I was happy and that this life I had fallen into was enough for me. But I really wasn't – and once I realised that, I knew that sooner or later I had to do something about it.'

Jamie now works as a journalist in London. He came for a three-week vacation but then decided he just couldn't go back. He quit his job over the phone: 'My boss was a friend of my dad, so it really didn't go over well back home. To rub salt in the wound, I had just been given a pretty big promotion.' But Jamie has no doubt it was the right decision. This way, he had no choice but to stick it out. It was terrifying, but in the end, it's the most freeing thing he's ever done, he tells me. All the weight he had been carrying around for years without knowing it, the expectations of his family and career, just melted away. For the first time in ages, he felt happy, serene. And he knew he needed to hold on to that feeling, no matter what.

Whereas a career in journalism always felt out of his reach in Sydney, Jamie quickly made connections in the industry in London and was able to build one there. A writer he met in a pub in Hackney helped him get some work experience at the *Sunday Times*, where he was eventually hired for a full-time position. 'Working as a real journalist! In London! I couldn't believe it!'

But perhaps the biggest change for Jamie was being able to fully come out of the closet as a gay man. He had come out to his friends, his mother and siblings a few years earlier, but just couldn't tell his father. 'He comes from a religious background and, although he drinks alcohol and hardly ever goes to the mosque, still identifies as Muslim. For him, it was a cultural issue more than a religious one. How would he explain his gay son to his family? It would be too much for him. So I put it off. Even after I told everyone else in my life, I couldn't tell him.'

In Sydney, Jamie lived in constant fear that he would be identified by one of his father's colleagues or employees while he was out. 'I used to skulk around in the night like a rat, never able to relax unless I was in some dark basement club where nobody could recognise me. I would never be able to hold a guy's hand or kiss him in public. I had regular nightmares about being found out. Completely paranoid. Eventually, it just got to be too much. I just stopped going out, stopped meeting guys, even stopped hanging out with my gay friends. I just turned my whole sexuality off. I went into self-induced celibacy and lived like a monk.' When he thinks back to it now, it makes Jamie truly sad. He had just come out of the closet, one of the hardest things he ever did. As he sees it, he should have been out celebrating and exploring this new side to himself. But he just couldn't.

On the other side of the world in London, away from anyone he or his family knew, Jamie could finally feel comfortable living his life as a gay man. 'I got on the apps, I went out, and I joined some gay meetups. I wasn't scared to show my face any more. I even fell in love and got in my first relationship. I was twenty-seven but it was like I was a teenager. It didn't work out, but that's not the point. I'm finally moving. I spent years in Sydney stuck in my own fear and confusion. I feel like I'm finally living my life.'

Would he do it all over again? 'Absolutely. I never realised how much baggage I was walking around with until I did. I had a thousand little voices in my ear all the time, telling me to do this, to be that. Getting away from it all, I could finally hear my own voice. It was like going from a room with a hundred radios playing at the same time to silence. It was a shocking process, but I've learned so much about myself. Now when I go back home and the music turns back up, I can still hear myself amid the tumult.'

•◆•

It was another kind of tumult, the pressure to conform to her middle-class Chinese parents' vision of success, that drove Lulu, a young woman from mainland China, to leave home. It wasn't until she managed to move to Singapore on a scholarship that she was able to find friends (and eventually a husband) who thought in the same way she did.

Like Natsuno and Jamie, Lulu Chang grew up in a loving family, but at some point started feeling that she didn't belong where she had grown up. Hers was a typical middle-class setting in the eastern Chinese province of Anhui. Lulu's father is a teacher, her mother, a nurse. They are among the 250 million Chinese people who have migrated internally in recent decades to seek a better life. She was a shy, introverted teenager, lacking confidence and with few friends. As in the case of many nomads, reading was Lulu's first form of travel; it made her want to go out there and see the world. She read *Jane Eyre* and *The Catcher in the Rye*, and was particularly inspired by *On the Road*: 'I realised it only in hindsight, but the seeds of my international aspirations were planted by Jack Kerouac.'

Lulu's parents worked hard to offer her the best education they could. She performed very well in school, with the unintended consequence of raising their hopes for her still further. This led to a sense of having heavy expectations placed on her shoulders from a young age. Like many young, middle-class Chinese people, her parents had fixed ideas of what would make her happy and, more importantly, successful. 'People in China can have a rather rigid mindset [about success],' she explains. 'When you're a student, you're expected to work hard and get top grades. From there you go to a top university in China and then go on to do a Master's overseas in the US, UK or somewhere in Europe. Then you get a stable job, get married – ideally before you're thirty – have kids and buy a house. If you've made it there, you've reached the top.'

Lulu diligently followed the pathway set out for her. She studied hard and excelled in her classes. 'I was a good daughter and a really good student. My life was study and family. I wasn't exposed to anything else.' But under her cool exterior, Lulu was beginning to question whether the life she was pursuing would make her happy. When she moved to an elite private school for her university entrance exams, her crisis reached a melting point. 'I kept asking myself: "What am I studying for? It's not going to apply to anything in my life, and it's not going to teach me anything valuable." I was really unhappy.' After two years, she had gone from the top of the class to the bottom.

When she was in primary school, one of Lulu's close friends had won a scholarship to study in Singapore. At the time, that didn't look like a desirable option. 'I thought, as we were taught in China, that Singapore was small, irrelevant. I wanted to aim higher. Why study in Singapore when you can go to the US or Europe?' But she reached out to her friend, who convinced her it could be a stepping stone to somewhere or something else. She also emphasised how much more liberal the approach to life was there compared with mainland China. That settled it for Lulu. She decided to apply for a scholarship, and she got in.

Lulu moved to Singapore one month before turning eighteen and went through a period of culture shock and paradoxical emotion. In China, her whole life had been laid out for her in regimented fashion. Living abroad without her family was liberating, but her first two years were spent mostly with fellow Chinese students from the mainland who all carried the same expectations from their parents: study hard, find a well-paid job and settle down (meaning get married). Lulu wasn't impressed. 'I still felt like I was living someone else's life.' One day, she took the time to sit down and write what her ideal life would look like: 'A job I truly enjoyed, good friends and real connections, self-love, serenity and the opportunity to learn about the whole world,' was the list she came up with. This exercise allowed Lulu to see that if she continued on her current trajectory, she would not achieve anything of the sort. She had little confidence in herself and felt she didn't know who she was. Something needed to change.

Lulu remembered Kerouac and, inspired by her reading, travelled as much as she could throughout university. She spent her first summer holidays working at SeaWorld in

Orlando, Florida. The following year she spent two months in Turkey working at a summer camp for a local high school. Most of the time, she travelled alone and did a lot of couch surfing. She started to grow as a person, and to understand who she really was, what she liked and disliked. She learned to embrace change – to expect the unexpected, to grab every opportunity that life threw her way. That turned out to be empowering. It allowed her to overcome her fear of expressing her uniqueness. 'I built up my confidence little by little, applying what I learned travelling to every aspect of my life. I know how to handle the ups and downs and embrace those tough moments now. And it has made me better and stronger as a person.'

After returning from one of her trips, she began dating Mike, a British IT engineer working in Singapore. 'I met him through mutual friends in Singapore at a time when I was least expecting a serious relationship.' Two-and-a-half months later, Lulu got down on one knee and proposed to him. I ask if her trajectory as a nomad played a role in enabling her to challenge conventions regarding gender roles. 'Definitely, yes,' she answers without missing a beat. 'He was about to relocate to Dubai, and I felt like if I didn't pop the question, I might regret it. So I mustered the courage to do it.' It was an impulsive decision, but the two are still happily married after nearly four years.

Lulu's new-found confidence also changed her relationship with her parents. Until she started working, she carried a lot of guilt and resistance towards them. They felt she was being selfish for travelling instead of visiting them, or for

changing jobs without a solid plan. Her spontaneous marriage has helped settle some of the tensions she experienced
with them. 'They can't really communicate with Mike that
much, but they can tell he's a caring guy and that has brought
them relief.'

Lulu firmly believes things are meant to happen for a
reason. She's also an existentialist who believes that we
make our own destiny. She has a message for young people
everywhere who feel trapped behind mental bars back home:
'You can do it. It won't be easy. It won't work out the way
you planned it – it never does. But whatever the outcome,
sooner or later, you'll find it was all worth it. Even if you end
up having to reverse course and you momentarily feel like a
failure for it, that feeling will pass. What you've learned will
stay with you for life.'

Recently, Lulu completed her yoga teacher training in
India and has been working for a company that helps food
and beverage businesses reduce food waste. This feels right
to her. She is in a good place.

•◆•

Liberals tend to think of the common form of Othering that
is labelling and stereotyping as a thing racists and bigots
do. The story of Thomas Chatterton Williams, the African
American author who settled in Paris, is a sobering reminder
that Othering is not only something the far right does, and
shows how easily one can go from being the victim of racial
prejudice of one kind to experiencing another.

Thomas has been living in France since 2011 with his

French wife and two kids. And even if his French is still halting, it has been a liberating experience. In France he can live not as a Black man but as an American – something he rarely experienced back home. 'In the US, you have to be on the team. The Black team, the white team, the Democrat team, the Republican team. Most of the time, I just feel thankful to be in Europe and to have distance from that kind of forced madness, forced identity politics. Here I feel I can claim the right to be an individual, maybe because I'm not French. Living away from home allows you to exist on your own terms in a way that you can never at home,' Thomas argues, echoing the feelings of the nomads in the opening chapter of this book.

Thomas started writing about these feelings from Paris and immediately took flak from people accusing him of being elitist. He was accused of being selfish and ignoring the plight of African Americans. Critics pointed out that moving to Paris was a luxury that few African Americans could afford. Having left the US because of the racism he experienced as a Black man, among other reasons, Thomas found that his departure was being held against him and that he was castigated as a kind of sell-out by a number of self-styled woke activists and intellectuals back home.

'People said: "How is Michael Brown going to move to Paris?!"[4] Of course I understand that not everyone is in a position to do that, to free themselves that way. But more people are than we tend to think. And if you could do that, why wouldn't you take the possibility seriously? I feel I have liberated myself in many ways from the American racial binary and that could not have happened if I'd stayed in the States.'

Thomas finds inspiration in the story of the American novelist Richard Wright, a self-described 'native born American Negro', who in 1951 started his incredibly powerful manifesto *I Choose Exile* with the following controversial lines: 'The first thirty-eight years of my life were spent exclusively on the soil of my native land. But, at the moment of this writing, I live in voluntary exile in France and I like it. There is nothing in the life of America that I miss or yearn for. Barring war or catastrophe, I intend to remain in exile. I shall, of course, keep my American citizenship, my American passport; but I prefer to live out my days among a civilized people.'

For Thomas, what Wright expresses beautifully in that text is that every moment you spend fighting for your freedom is a moment you're not free. 'At some point, having spent his life in America fighting for the rights of the Negro people and knowing that that fight was, morally and legally, a correct one, Wright decided that he was done fighting.' I respect that. He also rejects the essentialisation of Blackness that requires each and every African American to swear allegiance to the Black tribe or be castigated as a sell-out. For him, the idea that Obama was the best thing that ever happened to Black America is as ludicrous as the idea that Trump is the worst.

Thomas wrote a memoir, *Losing My Cool*, on what he regards as the destructive influence of hip-hop culture on young Black men. These days he is best known for his public dispute with Ta-Nehisi Coates, one of the champions of Black identity politics in America, making him a favourite target of left-wing intellectual circles. Thomas finds Coates' overarching contention that everything bad in the United States can be explained by the original sin of slavery, and the oppression of Blacks by whites, simplistic and characteristically American. And that the only way to fully understand this is for African Americans to put distance between America and them, if only for a while: only then will it become clear that American Black culture, by claiming Blackness as the main prism through which to look at America and indeed everything in the universe, has led African Americans to the characteristically (white) American notion that they are American before they are human.

I asked Carl Davis, another African American from a lower middle-class background who moved to Tanzania to flourish as an entrepreneur, what he thought about the dispute. 'I'm not surprised,' Carl told me. 'In the US, you have to identify with certain expectations. My story is that I was neither considered Black enough by my Black friends nor good or white enough by everyone else. Here in Africa, I'm American, I'm a businessman, but most important to me, I'm a person, not a skin colour. I'm grateful for that. I'm not saying there is no merit in fighting for Blackness. I'm saying young Blacks in the US should be encouraged – and financed – to get out and see what it feels like not to be first and foremost Black.'

This chimed with the feeling another Black American, Solomon Hughes, once described to me: 'The first time I walked on an African street, I experienced something I had never experienced before: not having to worry about keeping my distance from others or the potentiality of being perceived as a threat by white folks. It was a deeply liberating, life-altering moment for me. I wish every Black American could get a taste of that, at least once.'

For Carl, too, it was one of the most freeing experiences he ever had. He continued: 'It probably wouldn't hurt for African Americans to see Africans be racist, too. Black Americans think white America is particularly, obscenely racist. Having lived here for a while, I've seen enough racism to know it's not American or African. Racism is a form of fear and fear is human.'

In 2015, Thomas wrote a column in *The New York Times* entitled 'The Next Great Migration'.[5] In it, he argued that in light of the horrifying racism Blacks continue to face in America – to this day, they are twenty-one times more likely than whites to be shot by the police in the United States – perhaps it was time for them to consider migrating. He wrote that they should move to places 'that allow Black expats the status – still too often denied in America – of being treated first and foremost as Americans and not as Blacks'. It is ironic that the shocking, condescending way Africans and Blacks of African descent are often treated in France, especially when they live on the other side of the *périph*, the highway which separates downtown Paris from the *banlieue*, is at least somewhat lost on him.

·◆·

Natsuno, Lulu and Thomas each had their own reasons for leaving. For Natsuno, it was freeing herself from patriarchy and living her African dream. For Jamie, it was about transcending professional boundaries and exploring his

115

sexuality. For Lulu, it was about following her dreams rather than conforming to those of her parents. For Thomas, it was about escaping a society that viewed his phenotype as his paramount defining feature.

For Charlotte, it was about escaping the suffocating French bourgeoisie.

Growing up in Le Vesinet, a posh suburb of Paris, Charlotte de Casablanca had all the accoutrements of an aristocratic lifestyle. The women of her parents' set lived in large, gated homes, were members of the opera society and drank their lunches in chic Parisian restaurants. Charlotte was destined to join their ranks from birth. Her life was to be lived amid plush velvet sofas and the tinkle of crystal wine glasses. But Charlotte felt something was off.

Many girls would have done anything to be part of that world. But for her, it was a golden cage. So she escaped and left the country. Her odyssey led her to Slovenia and Turkey, and from there, to Canada, Bahrain, India and Mexico. But it was in Bogotá, Colombia that she decided to settle down and to become native in her own, personal, unique way. Charlotte reinvented herself as a singer and an actress in the process. Like my mother, the New Yorker in Paris, her identity is all about being a French artist in Bogotá, and her *nom de scène* reflects this: La Sirena Francesa. The French Mermaid has beautiful red hair and a sparkle in her eye. When she speaks and when she sings, with or without her cover band the Barracudas, her presence fills the room.

Charlotte's childhood was plagued by domestic drama. Some of her earliest memories are of her parents fighting.

Nonetheless, she speaks fondly of that time. Her father was an entrepreneur and inventor. He designed the Dallas, a small, easy-to-handle four-by-four car very popular in the Caribbean, and the Chef Express, an oven that could defrost foods at lightning speed. Her mother, meanwhile, was a free spirit whose life was a tapestry of wild romances. For a short while she worked as a model but 'never had the willingness or latitude to develop a career of her own'. She met Charlotte's father in Paris and settled into the comfortable life of an aristocratic housewife.

Charlotte grew up surrounded by the narrow, old-fashioned assumptions and pressures of that background. 'My dad is from an aristocratic family, and for him, there was no question that my mum would just sit at home and be happy.' Her future was all mapped out for her. 'I was supposed to marry someone from my class and become a housewife.' A housewife means very different things depending on culture and milieu, so I ask Charlotte what that would have meant for her. She takes a minute to think about it. 'A life of intellectual idleness and endless, mindless gossiping, I guess. Gossiping sounds benign, but it is a form of bullying which can be incredibly violent and destructive.'

She understood from a young age that the best way to get out of this suffocating environment was to do well in school, and she worked hard to be at the top of her class. Her dad took the helm of a small hotel chain and the family moved to Cannes, where her mother was from and where one of the hotels was located. Life on the Riviera was in many ways dreamlike, but also parochial, and before long, Charlotte found the cocooned existence she led there as suffocating as life in Le Vesinet. After her baccalaureate, she attended the Bordeaux branch of Sciences Po, and in 2004 spent her first long spell abroad in Slovenia, just after the country joined NATO.

This period was dominated by the pressures of trying to maintain her relationship with her boyfriend in Paris. The back and forth took its toll and she took the painful decision to end the relationship. Like Jamie, at some point Charlotte realised she needed to leave her family's plans for her behind in order to become the person she wanted to be. She says she 'just didn't know how to do that without leaving the country'.

Charlotte graduated in 2009 – at the height of reverberations from the financial crash. 'The times lent themselves to leaving. Opportunities weren't looking so bright in France. One of my greatest assets was that I spoke three languages. So, I started to look for things abroad.'

That is how her career as a trade journalist covering energy in Istanbul started. 'I never thought my career would begin this way, but I knew when I applied that I could totally pull it off. The job matched my personality, and I saw it as a door opening to something shiny and wonderful. I'd expected to land a job in France first and then, when I was more mature, make the jump abroad. But it happened differently, and it was perfect.'

From Istanbul, Charlotte was sent all around the world on four- to six-month assignments. She discovered India and Canada and eventually landed in Mexico, her first experience of Latin America. It was a revelation. She loved everything: the parties, the shiny, colourful culture, the Latin hyperbole. After one more short assignment in Bahrain, she and two colleagues decided to set up their own business, and her seven months in Mexico made her look closely at Latin America for a potential base. A law relating to publishing houses in Colombia meant they wouldn't have to pay taxes until 2023 if they set up shop there. They picked the country mainly for that reason, but what Charlotte found here was more important: 'Behind the superficial image featuring only drug cartels and the FARC, there is so much more to Colombia. Imagine reducing the US to Trump, McDonald's and the NRA ... Gabriel García Márquez and magical realism did not come from nowhere. Colombians are elegant, highly cultivated people. And life here is relatively inexpensive.'

I ask what her life would have been like if she had stayed in France. 'Definitely less interesting! Being a foreigner has shaped a lot in my career. I'm considered exotic here. It really appeals to people, whether in business or the arts.' Charlotte doubts she would have had the chance to develop her real-life or artistic skills in France. 'I began acting here at twenty-eight, completely randomly. Of course, it was a luxury made exponentially possible by my being a French woman in Colombia. In France, acting is a lot about hobnobbing and nepotism.'

Bogotá is now Charlotte's home. Just as for Natsuno, Jamie and Lulu, the greatest gift of migration for Charlotte was freedom. It allowed her to redefine her identity, reinvent herself and become bold and fearless. Like Lulu, when she left her country, she had no clue what was going to happen. 'I made it, and I'm full of gratitude that I had the balls. What a gift! Maybe I always had it in me, but the fact that I migrated revealed it. When you've crossed the ocean, you can do anything,' she adds.

Charlotte believes there are some things all migrants share. 'It's the hope that you're going to get something out of it that looks better than what you have at home. You have to have faith in the universe to be a migrant. So many people tell you, "Don't go, you are crazy! You won't make it. If you do, you won't make your mark. It's too tough! The language barrier is too difficult." There's no shortage of naysayers. If you're willing to change your life, it takes inner strength to disregard all that. For me, migrating wasn't a matter of life and death, for sure. But I wouldn't have made it without faith.'

Does she have any advice for young people who like the idea of migrating but are afraid to do so? 'I would tell them that what makes them different and targets of scorn or ridicule could well become their biggest asset overseas. Being different is something they should cultivate. We all have weird things about us, things that distinguish us. Identify them and work on them to turn them into something interesting and attractive. The positive corollary of xenophobia is that there is often a fascination with the foreigner. The way that you position yourself will make who you are in the eyes of your hosts. It's not about re-writing your past or lying, but pushing forward the good things about yourself and emphasising them.'

What does all of this add up to? It shows that emigration provides opportunities for all of us, wherever we go. By gaining mental plasticity from their broader experience base, and coupling it to a society that suits them, migrants' lives are enriched. There is an obverse side to this coin, too. Viewing immigrants not as visitors to your place, but as leavers from theirs, is a subtle, nuanced difference, but, perhaps, an important one. In Britain, people may gripe about immigrants who, as it is (probably apocryphally) said, 'come here and take our jobs'. But they would do well to remember that plenty of Britons go elsewhere to take up appointments and seek opportunities. As I said, emigration and immigration are linked – there is a constant circulation of leavers and newcomers, a kind of grand version of a school exchange system. No patriotic Briton would want to see a fellow countryman suffer xenophobia and abuse abroad. If that's the case, we would all be wise to remember the golden rule – 'treat others as you wish to be treated.' Perhaps, though, the most important thing that emigration teaches is that where you come from and where you are going are pale shadows of life's real questions: who are you and who do you wish to become?

5

GET OUT!

We have seen the economic benefits of leaving, and the entrepreneurial spirit it fosters. Economics can operate as a pull factor, with migrants, often young, drawn to dynamic economies – be they traditional powerhouses like New York, or newer hubs such as Dar es Salaam. But economics, even in the prosperous West, is also a push factor. Just as for somebody like Natsuno in the previous chapter, a stifling atmosphere can push people out into the rest of the world, so too can a stifled economy.

Very often, when we hear the phrase 'economic migrant', we think of people on rafts heading to Europe across the Mediterranean. We think of people coming from the global South to the global North. But, as we are beginning to see, people are moving from everywhere to everywhere – North to South, South to South, North to North and North to South. As the economy becomes ever more connected, people can service it from wherever they are, and in different ways. This chapter will look at how, for some young people, a depressed economy is one that isn't working for *them*, rather than one that is officially in recession. We'll look at how, why and where that pushes them to migrate, and at the competition it has the potential to engender in their country of origin.

•••

I published my first proper op-ed in *Le Monde* the day before Obama's election in 2008. I wrote as an American from Paris, arguing that the 'Yes, We Can' presidency had the potential to relaunch the close strategic transatlantic partnership of the previous decades, and Franco-American relations in particular, after the Iraq War schism and the freedom fries years. My prediction fell flat – Obama was arguably America's first Pacific president, and President Sarkozy never got along with him as he did with George W. Bush – but that column launched my career as an occasional editorialist.

Six months after my epiphany in the radio studio, my ideas had had time to percolate. What started as an inkling about the potential value of travel and migration as a means to learn and grow had turned into a more explicitly political vision. France, as I saw it, was treating its youth unfairly. At 25 per cent, the rate of youth unemployment was double the rate of unemployment of the country as a whole. It had hovered around that level for three decades. I took this as proof of the fundamentally gerontocratic nature of the French political system and power structure. What if young people could not only grow and enrich themselves by leaving the country but also influence politics back home? After all, one thing no government or economy can do without is young people. To keep their jobs, politicians would have no choice but to put incentives in place to lure them back.

The time was ripe for a new salvo, a provocative yet thoughtful column on a very different subject from Franco-American relations. This time I was going to take on French elites, and I wanted to go for the jugular. I was not technically French, but, having grown up in Saint-Germain-des-Prés, I was very much part of the national elite that I sought to criticise. With this in mind, I reached out to my close friend the rapper Mokless, and to a TV presenter by the name of Mouloud Achour, both left-leaning children of North African immigrants from council estates. I sent them the column I had written and asked if they would co-sign it.

They were both game. Like me, they loved the idea of turning the issue of migration on its head and seeing it as an opportunity rather than the threat it was currently being portrayed as, in France and elsewhere. Our column, headlined with my expletive from the radio, *'Barrez-vous!'* ('Scram!'), ran in *Libération*, the daily founded by Jean-Paul Sartre in the wake of the 1968 student uprising, on the first day of the school year in September 2012. It argued that France had become a decrepit, over-centralised gerontocracy where elites had done little to reduce chronic youth unemployment. That a country that failed to pay attention to the needs of its youth was morally bankrupt. That it was time for young people to take matters into their own hands and hit the road.

We argued that if French youth took this idea on and acted on it, the ruling class would have to pay heed. Since the end of the three decades of sustained growth the French call

Les Trente Glorieuses, which came to a close in 1975, France had been barely plodding along economically. If the young, the lifeblood of the nation, took off, their whole future at the top of the pyramid was in question.

The column created a stir and upset a lot of people, to my utter delight. By noon on the day it ran, I was busy doing the rounds on the daily talk shows. I had been a talking head on TV and the radio on a variety of issues for a few years by then, but this took things to a whole new level. In the ensuing days, politicians of every stripe were asked for their views on our manifesto. Predictably, with a few exceptions, most reactions were hostile. Jean-Marie Le Pen, the patriarch of the French far right, told journalists that 'Mouloud, instead of encouraging French youth to leave, should tell his "cousins" to stop coming to France'. On the set of one talk show, the head of General Electric in France told me she regarded French youth who stayed as the Resistance, which left little doubt as to how she felt about those who might be tempted to leave. Britain isn't the only country in Europe where the Second World War is a source of dubious imagery.

While we had relished being deliberately provocative, it did come back to bite us. We had grabbed the country's attention, but the national conversation we had started soon got stuck on a single point. We must hate France. We started getting interview requests from abroad and *The Times* of London, always happy to indulge in a little French-bashing, ran a story entitled 'Get out while you can, says Monsieur Scram'. This was doing nothing to dispel the impression that our beef was with France. Media from the US, China,

Germany, Brazil, Italy, Spain, the Netherlands, Croatia and even Australia followed suit.

In the summer of 2013, President François Hollande was asked about our movement on prime-time television. He was confronted with the story of a graduate of Sciences Po – the Grandes Écoles, again, always – who had to move to Australia because she couldn't find a job. Hollande was faced with a blunt question: 'What would you say if you had a young person in front of you who couldn't find a job and who was losing hope?' Hollande's answer was flaccid at best, a denial of reality at worst. 'I'd tell this young person that France is your country. This country loves you,' he replied, as if simply repeating the old line that France had more to offer would make it true. 'My duty is to tell this young woman it's here in France that you must succeed.'

This television appearance did not go down well (one of Hollande's key advisors got the boot immediately after for sending him on the show unprepared), and the *New York Times* asked me to write a piece about Hollande's comments.[1] I seized the opportunity to make the argument an economic one, pointing out that duty to your place of birth does not supersede creating opportunity and innovation. But the broader international response the article generated made me realise something crucial.

France's issues with growth and youth unemployment were real. But things were (and still are) even worse in many other places around Europe, like Italy, where young people were three times less likely to land a job than the broader population, not to mention the Arab world or Africa, where stifling gerontocracy is the norm. My focus, because I was there, was France's flaws. But the dismay of young people is a global phenomenon, not a French exception. What was needed was a way to find out how young people were doing globally. And so I cooked up a new idea: that of the Youthonomics Global Index (YGI), a ranking of countries according to youth-friendliness.

I hired a young economist to compile and analyse a whole range of data sets pertaining to young people around the world. The YGI came out in 2015, ranking sixty-four countries across fifty-nine different criteria, from youth unemployment rates, quality and cost of education, access to technology and entrepreneurship all the way to political representation, the ability of young people to afford housing and save for the future, religious freedom and even suicide rates.

In many countries, we found there was no longer a net transfer of wealth from parents to children.[2] Yet younger generations were still expected to finance the retirement of their elders through social security deductions from their pay and taxes, with the financial arrangements for their own retirements currently in a state of flux. Exacerbating the issue, in the wake of successive financial crises, baby-boomer politicians had opted to take billions (perhaps trillions) in worthless debt accumulated by hedge funds, pension funds, banks and other private financial institutions and convert that into public debt, thereby effectively passing the burden on to their grandchildren and great-grandchildren.

Throughout the world, this had made the young dispro- portionately poorer. But the implication of the Youthonomics index confirmed my inkling that the boot was now on the other foot. Unprecedented international mobility gave the young unprecedented leverage. By voting with their feet – moving from one country or city to another, as well as, as we will see, from the city to the countryside – the young can turn the world into a beauty contest between cities, countries and regions vying to attract them. In many countries – although not all – where the young are either ignored, manipulated, patronised or downright mistreated, they are increasingly deploying a potent new weapon: leaving.

In the YGI, wealthy and relatively progressive countries with smaller populations like Denmark, Sweden, Norway, Switzerland, New Zealand and Canada ranked towards the top, which was hardly surprising. Young people want to see good levels in education, health and well-being, employment and opportunity, and chances for youth political and civic participation, and these countries fare well on all these measures. Countries with gerontocratic traditions like France, Japan, Italy and Spain performed relatively poorly. A growing number of young people in those countries are taking advantage of technology to try and build the foundations of a life abroad.

Take Deborah, her brother Victor and their friend Mirian. They are from Madrid and moved to the UK, settling together in the northeast of London in 2014. 'In Spain, even with work experience, motivation and self-confidence, I wasn't getting anywhere,' Deborah confides. 'There, it's all about who you know.' I'm well-placed to realise that knowing the right people helps everywhere, but I see what she means. With the chutzpah this young woman exudes, she should have been well able to thrive in her own country. She continues: 'I don't want to live in a place that doesn't value me. Instead of complaining, Victor, Mirian and I took action to change our fate. We packed our bags and hit the road. But London is a hard place to live sometimes. As a Mediterranean, you can feel lonely and isolated here. Thank God we have each other.'

I met these three thanks to an app that connected dog owners with dog sitters. I had had mixed experiences using such marketplaces and so I tried them out, placing Watson and Sherlock under their care. By the way they wagged their tails when we arrived to collect them from the Spanish home, I could tell my two fellows had enjoyed their time there.

In 2014, youth unemployment in Spain hit a startling 57 per cent. Upon hearing their story, I remember trying to imagine how tough it must have been for the siblings and their friend to move to a grinding metropolis like London where everything was three or four times more expensive than back home. After a while, Deborah and Victor were hired by a sushi company and the assertive Deborah was soon promoted to branch manager. Last time I spoke to her, she was managing a juice and smoothie bar, Victor was training alongside her and Mirian, who was studying marketing, occasionally came by to wait tables. 'Was it worth it? Would you recommend leaving your place of birth to others?' I ask them. 'Definitely. Just do it! There is always the possibility to go back home if things don't work out. In the meantime, the way you will have grown, the things you will have learned, the experiences you will have made, the places, people and cultures you will have discovered ... all those things are priceless.'

In the YGI, Norway topped the list, in no small part due to its flexible labour market. Norway is also not afraid of its young citizens crossing its borders to find work. In fact, Norway shares employment data with neighbouring Sweden, and when there is no job for a young person in one country, the government will fund their trip to interview for an open position in the other. This is quite the opposite of what we saw in France, with the government telling young people it was their duty to stay. The US and UK didn't do that well either. But perhaps the single most surprising trend underscored by the ranking was that China, and to a lesser extent India, showed a new capacity to project soft power, and were attracting young people in particular. Compared to southern European countries such as Portugal, Spain and Italy, China was more attractive.

I wanted to find out more about these results. What, apart from unemployment, is driving young people out of southern Europe, and what does China have in common with Norway?

•◆•

The bullet train between Shenyang and Dalian in China leaves as often as fifty times each day. The journey of just under 400km can take as little as an hour and a half, depending on where the train stops, which makes it significantly faster than the 350km journey from London to Liverpool, at a third of the cost. It is the ideal means of transport for professionals who commute between the two cities for work.

It was such a train that Ismaila Barry boarded in October 2014 during Golden Week, the national holiday instituted in 1999 to grow domestic tourism by allowing the rising Chinese middle class to make long-distance family visits. As he slowly made his way to his seat through the crowded carriage, he hardly noticed that he was an attraction. Ismaila had picked the slow train by mistake and decided to take a nap once he realised the journey would take four hours. He was woken up halfway there by a commotion just in front of him. As he opened his eyes, he was faced with a crowd of locals busily taking pictures of him. As he awoke fully, dumbfounded, they kept on taking photos, some shamelessly posing in the frame thanks to elaborate selfie sticks, without showing the slightest hint of embarrassment.

The defining feature that made Ismaila Barry worthy of such unwanted attention? His skin was black.

In many other countries, such behaviour would be considered offensive. In fact, in most other countries it wouldn't happen at all. But China is not every country, and it plays by its own rules – especially when it comes to race. 'China isn't more racist than other places,' Barry told me. 'People with black skin are just a rarity in China. The way people behaved around me sometimes when I first arrived to study, especially when I left the campus and urban environments, made me super uncomfortable. I had never encountered the kind of ethnocentrism I have experienced here anywhere else, to be sure. But living in China also made me realise that what I might have called "racism" before was just an unfiltered reaction to the odd, the strange, the foreign in a country that is fundamentally inward-looking. As an African, learning that did me a lot of good.'

I first met Ismaila Barry, an expressive, fit young man with a cheerful smile and nascent beard, at the Soumbédioune fish market in Dakar in the spring of 2018. We had started talking while he was still in Shanghai; he happened to be visiting his family while I was in town. The sun was beginning to set, and the fishermen were busy selling their catch of the day, surrounded by *pirogues*, the elegant, multicoloured fishing boats ubiquitous here. Ismaila was sporting a flashy T-shirt, black trousers, brand-new sneakers and aviator sunglasses.

Ismaila's parents are both Senegalese, and both got scholarships to study behind the Iron Curtain in the 1980s. His dad, Boubakar, studied nuclear physics in Dresden, then East Germany, and spent ten years there in total. His mother, Medinatou Mohamed Diop, who grew up in Kaolack, a small city just north of Senegal's border with The Gambia, won a scholarship to study hydrological and geological engineering in what was then Czechoslovakia. 'My parents were both from very humble backgrounds, self-made. My dad helped his mum every morning by carrying her tables to the market, and only then was he allowed to go to school. At night, he had to go out to study under street lighting – there was no electricity at home.'

I paid Boubakar Barry a visit to find out why he came back to Senegal when so many of his generation did not. He is now an esteemed, somewhat feared physics professor at Cheikh Anta Diop University in the centre of Dakar, and has quite the reputation. From the slightly alarmed look of the students who gave me and my son, who was tagging along, directions to get to his office, it was obvious he doesn't suffer fools lightly. He told me, 'My future wife and I were pan-Africanists. We felt our rightful place was participating in Africa's rise, and to do so from Africa.'

After they made their way back to Senegal, Boubakar and Medinatou immediately started working. She took an engineering job at the SOCOCIM, a cement plant. Soon the couple co-created INTELECT, a computing and electronics distributor and consulting firm. Medinatou moved on to manage a department at the state-owned pharmaceutical distribution company, her present occupation.

The couple had three children, all of whom they pushed hard at school. During school breaks, when other children were out on the streets playing, Ismaila and his brothers were forced to stay inside and study. 'My dad didn't want us to be good. He wanted us to be excellent.' Thanks to his job at the university, Boubakar was one of the first people in the country to have a home computer. This gave Ismaila and his siblings an advantage over fellow students at school.

At the age of eleven, Ismaila saw pupils from his future school parading on Senegal's National Day. He'd never heard of the place before but was taken with the school uniforms. 'Dad told me that if I wanted to do that, I'd need to study very hard.' Ismaila got the message and was eventually admitted to the school, where he met Abdi, whom we met in the introduction, just arrived from Mali. From there, he undertook management studies and soon figured out that he needed to study abroad. 'No one speaks English in Senegal, and I was beginning to understand that I needed to,' he told me. He applied and was admitted to the prestigious University of Cape Coast in Ghana.

As is the case for many other young nomads, this first proper experience abroad was a formative one for Ismaila, a key stepping stone on his way to China. For people who haven't visited a different continent, the difference between various countries within it remains quite theoretical. But as any European student who spent a year abroad in Europe thanks to the Erasmus exchange programme can attest, even within the same region, cultural differences can be unsettling. Berlin is not Burnley. That feeling of being a fish out of water made Ismaila grow faster. Ghana and Senegal are actually quite far apart (roughly the distance between London and Kiev). Ghana is a Christian-majority country; Senegal is overwhelmingly Muslim. But the most interesting difference for Ismaila lay elsewhere.

The British influence left over from the colonial era meant Ghana was a world away for him: 'The mentality is so different to the French-speaking African countries! Ghanaians are traders; they have amazing business acumen. I wasn't used to that entrepreneurial spirit at all,' he explains. Indeed, Ghana's economy is far more robust, three times the size of Senegal's. The French influence in Senegal can be seen in the country's reverence for engineers, embodied in recent years by President Macky Sall, a graduate of the French energy engineering school IFP. But while France's inclination for technocracy is often counterbalanced by lyricism, that's not the case in Senegal. While the Parisian Champs-Elysées was named after the Greek mythological heavens, the equivalent found on Senegal's island of Gorée is known simply as the VDN, which stands for *Voie de Dégagement Nord* (North Clearing Way).

For Ismaila, what was most striking was that archaic traditions, ethnic affiliations, fellowships and red tape seemed far less prevalent in Ghana. 'In Senegal, if you have a business idea, people tell you "Oh, no, that won't work, it's too risky, you're too young!" When I talked to people, to business owners, to mentors in Ghana, everything seemed possible.'

Discovering the transformative power of migration within Africa made him curious to find out what would happen should he leave the continent. But unlike many of his fellow students who were dreaming of Europe and America, Ismaila had his sights on a different part of the world. His whole life, he had witnessed France's diminishing influence in Senegal and the rise of China's. In Ghana, he realised this was not about Senegal alone. China was building up its presence everywhere in Africa. In 2014 his university started offering Chinese courses.

Ismaila was already interested in Asia (he had been studying Japanese for three years because of a childhood passion for samurai movies and for anime and manga), but the hype about China kicked his imagination into high gear. 'I wasn't aware of the One Belt One Road (OBOR) initiative itself,' he recalls, referring to the mammoth infrastructure, logistics and investment strategy adopted by the Chinese in 2014 to build up their global influence in the twenty-first century.

But, he says, 'the buzz about opportunities in China that motivated me to go there was all about OBOR.'

He thought Japanese lessons would give him at least a bit of a head start: 'Many Kanji characters you find in Japanese come from the Mandarin (*hanzi*), but Chinese is really much more complex.' Barry adds with a smile, 'I studied Mandarin non-stop for the next two years and I thought I was becoming quite good. I was in for quite the surprise.'

In 2015, Ismaila was selected by his university for a full-tuition scholarship financed by the Chinese government, part of China's effort to attract foreigners and especially Africans to study in China. Investing in soft power initiatives of this kind, as Beijing anticipates a growing need for African resources, makes perfect sense. The goal is to turn young African students into China enthusiasts the same way my father became enthusiastic about the US thanks to his Fulbright scholarship. Ismaila set off for Shanghai, and onwards to Liaoning.

China shook Ismaila to the core. The crowds, the buildings, the traffic, the number of people you would see on a single bike (up to five or six) or the amount of stuff trolleyed by one – everything was multiplied by ten, by a hundred. The city lights were brighter, the food spicier, the capitalism harsher. The northern Chinese weather provided another shock. One week, during his first winter there, the temperature fell to minus 32 degrees Celsius. 'In fact, winter there is so ruthless it is treated as a two-month holiday,' he explained to me.

He'd expected at least a few people to speak English and to

get by with everyone else in Chinese. But barely anyone spoke English – not even taxi drivers. More worryingly, the Chinese he had painstakingly learned at university was useless. 'No one understood me. I didn't realise it, but my mastery of the language was terribly academic.' He pauses and adds: 'Let me rephrase that. It was absolute shit.' In restaurants, Ismaila ended up having to mimic animals to explain which kind of meat he wanted. That didn't work out so well. As a Muslim, he was dismayed when he found out, after months of dining in one particular restaurant, that he had been eating pork because the waiters misunderstood his grunting. 'That story has become a classic back home. I'm forced to retell it every time I visit. They just can't stop laughing.'

While studying at Liaoning, Ismaila kept crisscrossing the country, taking in every little experience that he could, including being photographed by myriad strangers on the bullet train. One day, he was contacted by Hult, a Swedish business school, offering him a scholarship to study in Shanghai. That's how the city became his home the following year. In Shanghai, Ismaila improved his Mandarin and networked furiously, meeting people from all over the world, learning about different cultures.

Hult has multiple campuses globally, including one near the British Museum in Bloomsbury and one in San Francisco, so Ismaila got a taste of the UK and America during a semester spent perfecting his English. Ultimately, though, he opted to head back to Shanghai. 'I'd visited New York and London but, believe me, Shanghai is far more cosmopolitan!' he exclaims. 'The whole world is here!'

Back in China, Ismaila landed a job at SAE Asia, a Chinese logistics company, which didn't inspire him much but which he took because his student visa was about to expire. He found the Chinese work environment draining and, as an immigrant, particularly difficult. 'They really exploited me,' he said. Having hired him as a very junior sales rep, the company soon recognised his potential and offered him a role as their business development manager, but without increasing his salary. He decided to find another job. In a booming economy like China's, his unique pedigree, growing familiarity with the country and fluency in Mandarin allowed him to get a job as a consultant at Infratec, a German infrared technology company. He started off as a junior sales assistant, but within eighteen months was promoted to sales manager of the company's entire Chinese portfolio.

Ismaila's continued experience working in China has given him a first-hand understanding of how Chinese businesses operate. For many, on the outside, this knowledge makes him invaluable. He says that Chinese companies run on distinctive lines. Colleagues tend to be risk-averse and, despite the Chinese reputation for honesty and hard work, those qualities can be in short supply. 'It is very hard to make a decision because nobody wants to be responsible if something goes wrong. The result is a chronic lack of initiative. People react. They don't think ahead. I often end up making all the decisions. This gives me such headaches!' Ismaila also finds that more still than America, what makes China tick is money. 'In China, it's C.R.E.A.M. [Cash Rules Everything Around Me] all around,' he says in a nod to the most famous anthem of the Wu-Tang Clan, the Staten Island hip-hop band whose universe borrows heavily from kung fu cinematographic lore. 'It's all about the Maos.[3] It's a religion.'

Ismaila doesn't live in China anymore. When we last spoke, I wondered out loud if this had anything to do with China's treatment of Uighurs, but it didn't. 'I'm appalled by what's going on in Xinjiang [the region Uighurs originate from] and by the way Uighurs are discriminated against but not specifically as a fellow Muslim. It's a political problem. And there are many other pills one has to swallow to work in China. As a Muslim, I was able to practise my faith and celebrate religious holidays like Eid. Cops were even assigned to protect mosques around those times.'

Ismaila leveraged his expertise to get an excellent job in Europe, but what his experiences show is that dynamic or developing nations such as China capitalise on offering young people what they want. Education, job opportunities, not to mention the personal growth that we have already discovered that comes from being abroad – China has recognised their importance to youth and invested accordingly. Young or old, whether we migrate or not, education, job opportunities and personal growth are the key things dynamic people are on the lookout for. China's story of attracting young people through crucial investments has much to offer nations in the West that are stagnating.

•◆•

Another country that fared better than expected on the Youthonomics index was India. The nation's growth isn't as impressive as China's, and the rise of Hindu nationalism is tainting the conversation on immigration: the Citizenship Bill of 2016, which the ruling Bharatiya Janata Party (BJP) sought to turn into law in 2019, offers immigrants from Afghanistan, Pakistan and Bangladesh a path to Indian citizenship, as long as they are not Muslim. Still, in an unprecedented development, the country is seeing the children of Indians who migrated to the US, Australia and the Gulf countries return.[4]

Yassir, one such son of Indian emigrants, was born in Cleveland and grew up in Los Angeles – where for many years he introduced himself as a 'Cleveland Indian' in a facetious nod to the baseball team. When Yassir was ten, the family took him to India, and he hated everything about it. 'I didn't understand it. I thought it was dirty. It smelled. It was disgusting. I was your typical Californian brat coming from LA, where everything is sparkling clean. Suddenly, I was in a place without running water. I was like, "How do you not have a shower? How do you not have toilet paper? How do you not have all these things that are so basic and elementary?"' He couldn't understand why his parents would take him to such a terrible place and vowed never to return.

His parents worked tirelessly throughout Yassir's childhood and adolescence. Amir, his dad, was an architect. His mother Shahoor had grown up with servants and had been cast to star in what became a Bollywood classic, before being forced to marry Amir and migrate to the US. For her, having to work at all, let alone as a cleaning lady, as she did, was a sobering experience. As a result, Yassir, his sister Lia and brother Imraan were left to their own devices. Imraan kept getting into trouble and was a constant source of worry for the family. Yassir struggled through high school and barely got accepted into the University of California Santa Barbara, where he studied organic chemistry with the sinking feeling that it 'wasn't for me'. It was during his second year that he reluctantly agreed to return to India for a family reunion.

'It was like I was coming home,' Yassir recalls. 'All my dreadful memories of coming as a kid vanished at once. I was so grateful to have come back. One night, it was December 1997, the whole family was gathered in Pune for a party in a fancy hotel. At one point, I was standing outside smoking, when through the frame of the doorway, I saw my grandmother Bibijune, the family's warm-hearted matriarch, an extraordinary lady. She was sitting in the middle of a hundred people in a halo, and everyone was taking pictures of her ... I felt I was getting a glimpse of her aura. It's hard to explain, but through this vision of her, I suddenly felt awake and connected to the entire universe. It was like not knowing you can't see properly until you put on glasses. Everything came into clarity. I suddenly understood where I came from and where I wanted to go. And I started crying tears of joy. I finally got a side of me that I hadn't understood.' On the spot, Yassir decided he would move to India and live with his grandmother. The family didn't take his decision seriously and told him 'nobody goes from America to India'. But his mind was made up.

Back in California, Yassir got a job at a local ice cream parlour, despite them initially telling him they weren't hiring. 'I rejected their rejection and kept coming back until they relented. Working in that ice cream parlour was an awesome experience. I just loved every second of it. I was like a kid in a candy shop, experimenting with all the toppings, the fudges, the sauces, everything. People would just come in and say, "Yo, Yass, just make me whatever. I trust you." I'd have special flavours. Pumpkin ice cream was my secret ingredient.'

Yassir saved his earnings, dropped out of university temporarily, went to India for eight months and eventually moved there permanently, living with his grandmother, as he had dreamed of doing. Along the way, he trekked through the Himalayas and almost drowned while rafting on the Zanskar River in Kashmir, then nearly died again of thirst, hunger and exhaustion on a trek to Malana, an ancient Indian village in the state of Himachal Pradesh. In McLeod Ganj, headquarters of the Tibetan government-in-exile, he even met the Dalai Lama. 'He came out to meet us. We were just standing in line, everybody was crying, and he shook my hand. For me, it was the apotheosis of a spiritual journey. It left me with the feeling that if all this can happen to me, this scrawny kid from the suburbs of LA, nothing is impossible.'

'You know, Yassir, India needs good ice cream!' Nayyar, a gentleman he had met at a family wedding, told him when they met again in Bombay. Yassir was startled, and then realised he hadn't eaten ice cream for two years in India, except for kulfi (traditional Indian ice cream), because Western flavours and varieties were usually terrible. The following weekend they met again, this time at the city's Marriott Hotel, to discuss making ice cream together, when they noticed it had its own ice cream counter.

They took this as an omen of sorts and persuaded the hotel's *gelatiere* to allow Yassir to work in the hotel kitchen and learn about actually making ice cream. Now he could do much more than create fancy toppings as he had in LA. Meanwhile, he did his own little market study at a nearby branch of Baskin Robbins to get a sense of sales and customer flows. 'So there *was* American ice cream in India?' I ask. Yassir frowns: 'Sure. But they were doing everything wrong. It was like McDonald's for ice cream. I knew there was a niche for gourmet stuff.' Meanwhile, Nayyar travelled to Italy and persuaded an award-winning *gelatiere* in Liguria, Costanzo Malatto, to become a partner in the new business. It took some convincing, but in the end Malatto loved the idea of allowing a country of over a billion people to get a taste of his magic.

When it came to finding a name for the new venture, a self-described starry-eyed Yassir felt that 'Love is the answer to everything. So I jumped up, went to the computer, put the word into Google Translate and learned that the Italian word for love is *amore*. I said, "Ah, this is a nice word!" The name amoregelato.com wasn't taken. So I nabbed it. I said: "We're about love, and this will be the name." And that's how *Amore* started. We opened our first shop in Mumbai in 2006.'

Amore Gelato was an instant sensation. 'We were the first of our kind in Mumbai. Within six months, we had forty branches. By the end of the year, seventy.' Not everything went smoothly, though. Yassir and his colleagues were inexperienced and hit hard by swine flu, strikes, the terrorist attack on Mumbai, and the global crash of 2008. The

143

company went into debt and had tax problems, too. They were forced to cut back to twenty-five shops, but Yassir worked hard and eventually got the business back on track.

Success has followed success in Yassir's life in India. He built several related companies and in 2019 celebrated his fourth wedding anniversary. His wife Pari is an artist, actor and chef. His return to India has sparked a trend in the family. His mother followed him back and re-embraced acting. 'Truth is,' says Yassir, 'this whole place is like a giant theatre. It raises people's threshold of stimulation. Once you come here, nothing is the same afterwards. When I go back to America, I feel numb. Everything is too straightforward and laid out,' he exclaims. 'Here, everything is crazy. There are no set rules. That makes things difficult but exhilarating. India isn't efficient, but that is precisely what makes us incredibly resilient. Having started a business in India and succeeded, I know I can do it anywhere.'

Both Yassir and Ismaila felt as though their birthplaces were not able to provide them with the opportunities that would allow them to fulfil their potential, and therefore left. It may come as a surprise, but the American economy is not particularly kind to entrepreneurs. The 'employer enterprise birth rate', or the number of new businesses with at least one employee that emerge per year, is low in the United States when compared to other countries around the world. Countries as diverse as Switzerland, Mexico, Brazil and Sweden all outrank the US in this measure.[5]

While Yassir had the privilege of being born into a strong economy, it was not one that suited the kind of skills he had, and, judging by the kind of criteria that inform the Youthonomics Global Index, it was not attractive to him as a young person. India suited him better, precisely because 'there are no set rules'. With no place for his talents in the US, he moved somewhere they were in demand. Just as it was crying out for the product he sold, ice cream, the Indian marketplace is crying out for young people like Yassir. America, one feels, is saturated – both with ice cream vendors and with highly educated young people looking to get on in life.

For both Yassir and Ismaila, then, there was a push as much as a pull. They could certainly have made lives for themselves in the US and Senegal, but, for various reasons, the economies of these places were stagnant or unsupportive of their specific skills, personality types and goals. China and India, as emerging world superpowers, are courting young, entrepreneurial people and getting a great return on their investment as a result. The situation is good for the migrant – for Yassir or Ismaila – and good for the destination – China and India. Everyone's a winner.

Well, not quite. For there is, potentially, a loser also: in these cases, Senegal and the United States. No country wants to lose all of its talented young people. Perhaps countries with a youth migrant drain will be able to take counteracting measures quickly. In the twenty-first century, creating a nation that is attractive to young immigrants, by extension, means creating a nation that is attractive to young *people*. Perhaps, by taking a leaf out of Norway's book and becoming friendlier to the young, nations like the UK, the US and France can become more relaxed about their young moving

145

away. Firstly, they will have a counterbalancing influx of dynamic youth, and secondly, if they transform themselves back into attractive and dynamic countries, what Brits, Americans and French people learn abroad may well return at a slightly later date, carried home by the next generation.

In the United Kingdom, the university sector is heavily funded by international students, and Britain is enormously privileged to attract the world's richest among the brightest (poorer bright people tend to go elsewhere). In 2018, British institutions hosted 450,000 students from around the world, about two thirds of whom came from outside the EU. Yet, Britain, amazingly, has been at pains *not* to retain them. In 2012, as part of her 'hostile environment' policy, Theresa May, the home secretary at that time, clamped down on student visas. Historically, international students who attended UK universities had two years to find a job following their studies. May reduced this to four months. The result was that a record low of 6,300 individuals stayed in the country after their studies. Boris Johnson's administration reversed the policy in 2019, and so we may see greater numbers of young people staying in Britain after their studies. However, the first intake that this will affect is the coronavirus intake. It is a cliché, but the youth are the future. Any sane country should be at pains to attract young, dynamic people – not create a 'hostile environment' that pushes them away.

Both the *Barrez-vous!* movement and the Youthonomics Global Index were driven in part by good intentions: to help young people to flourish in what seemed like a world where the odds were stacking up against them. They hold lessons for many countries. But there is a way that they could also be seen as a form of intergenerational blackmail: 'Treat us right, offer us jobs and positions of power from a young age, or we'll bugger off to another, more welcoming land and leave you stranded.' By extension, there is potential to set up a confrontational, us vs them dynamic, one that is not simply generational, but rather split between the mobile and the static, the nomadic and the settled.

·◆·

While almost everyone can see the benefits of this form of migration in this chapter, with high-skilled workers travelling to find the best opportunities before, sometimes, taking that experience back to their country of origin, there is another form where returning home is impossible, and where our response has become much less helpful and clear: refugees. To read a liberal newspaper is to see refugees portrayed as utterly helpless individuals. To read a right-wing one is to see refugees presented as a potential fifth column, untrustworthy and parasitic.

But the earliest migrations of our species were likely forced, and the earliest migrants therefore refugees. Pushed by causes from climate change to overhunting, the earliest humans were forced to find new pasture to roam. It can't possibly be the case that all refugees are either helpless victims or mischievous, Machiavellian creatures, can it? What's happening behind the clichés? Who are the real refugees? And is there a more complex, and more positive, story to be told?

6

REFUGEES AND COMMUNITIES – '(DON'T) GO BACK TO WHERE YOU CAME FROM'

It was pitch dark, and Lamine Tounkara could barely see his companions as they made their way towards the beach. He had left his hometown of Tambacounda in Senegal five days before, travelling from town to town by bus before entering Mauritania at Rosso, a boring little border town basking in the Sahara sun, and then continuing by car and on foot through the mountains to the capital, Nouakchott. That's where he met the others. From there, new vehicles until they reached scrubland. Heading into the desert towards the Western Saharan border, they had to move more cautiously, at night and on foot. Lamine was never entirely sure where they were as they trod through the desert. Finally, he heard it – barely a murmur at first and then increasingly loud. Behind one last dune, the Atlantic Ocean appeared. They had made it this far. Now there was no turning back.

The promised *pirogues* turned out to be run-down craft

riddled with holes and equipped with barely functioning engines. But Lamine and his companions were feeling lucky. Many *piroguistes*, as the youngsters who risk their lives on rafts while trying to enter Europe are known in Senegal, are desperate enough to try to make it across by paddling. Braving the waves, they pushed the run-down *pateras* (as the rafts are known in Spain) into the sea, climbed in, got the motor running and immediately started bailing out with buckets to avoid sinking.

'I was excited but also scared shitless. Those were the most frightening moments of my life,' Lamine explained to me. 'It's the unknown that's the killer. We had only a vague idea of where we were heading and sat in water the whole way. We were hoping it was a "crossing", but the truth of the matter is that we were following vague instructions from the smugglers we had left behind in Western Sahara.' What seemed like an eternity later, in the early hours of the morning, Lamine's neighbour elbowed him with nervous excitement: 'Look, man! A seagull!' Ninety minutes later, they were on firm ground on the island of Gran Canaria, not far from Las Palmas. Lamine had made it to Spain. It was February 2003.

By the time Lamine landed in the Canary Islands, Africans had been risking their lives on rafts headed there for years. The first made it to the island of Fuerteventura in 1994 with two Sahrawi (Western Saharan) youths onboard. Year after year, month after month, the numbers kept growing. By 2003, several tens of thousands had tried their luck, many of them drowning on the way. The Cayucos crisis – named after the vessels that soon brought hundreds of people at a time – reached its peak in the following years. By 2007, patrols by the Spanish Civil Guard, repatriation agreements with the countries of the region, and news of Spain's Great Recession had steadily reduced the numbers of those attempting to make the crossing. Since 2008 there have been fewer than 1,000 migrants arriving in the Canaries each year.[1]

I met Lamine at Barcelona airport on a sunny spring day in 2018, fifteen years after he'd first set foot in Spain. He was standing among his cab driver colleagues outside the arrivals terminal. Most of them were sucking on Fortuna cigarettes. Not Lamine. With his elegant shades, perfectly cut chinos, immaculate white shirt and navy blue sweater, he stood out. He grinned when our eyes met, and laughed. We had been talking and texting for a couple of months and were thrilled to finally meet in person.

Lamine is larger than life. He's also caustic, and his sense of humour makes for a brilliant ice breaker. By the time we sat down at Hidden Café, a hipster establishment in Les Corts de Sarrià, formerly a village, now a trendy neighbourhood of the Catalan capital (moving borders, everywhere), so I could get my caffeine fix, I was busy thinking about how to tell his story. It is tempting to cast him as a hero. And so I started talking about his heroism. But he didn't like this one bit. 'I'm no hero, my friend. I didn't do this alone. *Hamdulillah* [Praise and gratitude for God], God was with me every step of the way. And then there were others. There were moments of intense loneliness of course, and I got screwed more than once by various people, including my own. But there were countless people, too, who helped me, almost every step of the way. My people here and back home, other Spaniards . . . And many others: Pakistanis, Germans, French dudes, you name it.'

Lamine is talking about something essential to the immigrant experience here, and one that is particularly important for refugees. Beyond the ability to read, write and count (which we should by no means take for granted as universal, even in rich countries), the most important currency of the nomad isn't money but the capacity to build bridges and hook up with others, to make acquaintances and friends: so-called networking skills. This is of particular necessity for refugees, because often it is the only currency that they have and that they can grow.

Of course, this is nothing new. What makes a good nomad is what makes a good human. We are social creatures at our core. This chapter, then, is about refugees, but it is also about networks and sociability. Refugees are so often portrayed as victims or perpetrators. What is less widely talked about is the refugee's reliance on and creation of networks. Put simply, you cannot travel across the world with no money without some help. Studies of toddlers show that they instinctively help people in need if they are able to.[2] The need for each other is part of our genetic make-up,[3] and regardless of age, our instinct is to move towards our peers, to seek and offer aid.

For migrants like Lamine, being able to rely on a network is a matter of survival. Migrating without money is almost impossible and extraordinarily perilous. But it can be just as perilous *with* money. Most of the refugees who fill the concentration camps that have popped up in Libya in recent years with the tacit support of the European Union have spent relative fortunes getting there, the reimbursement of which burdens their relatives back home for years, in many cases decades, only to see their hopes of migration dashed and their lives shattered by a combination of complex factors. Money can only get you so far. Without luck, acumen and above all a solid network of people he could count on upon arriving in Spain, not to mention an uncanny ability to get on with strangers, Lamine's journey would have been impossible.

Back in 2003, the Spanish Coast Guard picked up Lamine and his companions on the beach and took them to a refugee detention centre, where he stayed for around twenty days. Detainees from countries, like Senegal, that had signed repatriation accords with the Spanish were immediately deported. Lamine had grown up on the Ivory Coast, had Ivorian citizenship, and had knowingly thrown away his Senegalese passport. He received a document granting him asylum. This didn't allow him to work, but he was free. He was even asked where he would like to go in Spain. He chose to follow a group of thirty others who were flown to Murcia in the southeast of the country, since this option was readily available. Shortly after, 'cousins' in Barcelona sent him a bus ticket to join them there.

Like many Africans, Lamine ascribes a liberal meaning to words such as 'cousins', 'brothers and sisters', 'aunts and unks', 'mammas and papas'. More often than not, this actually means a friend he grew up with, say, or the mother of a friend. Sometimes it even just means a lady who lived with the family, helping with the kids and household chores in return for a seat at the family table and a mat to sleep on. This kind of solidarity is a daily fact of life in his world. The way Lamine sees it, 'It's our duty as Muslims, as Africans, as humans. Whenever possible, we help each other; we don't think twice about it.' For example, I ask: 'Were the Barcelonans who paid for your trip real cousins?' Sure enough, he replies, 'Well, friends of friends of an uncle, you know ... ' An extended kinship network is a cause and effect of nomadism; the nomad's sense of community is all the more steadfast for not being rooted in a single space.

Lamine didn't waste any time once he arrived in Barcelona. He immediately started learning Spanish and Catalan at a school for adults and volunteered at the town hall to help other immigrants find their bearings. 'As a newcomer, there was no better way to learn the dos and don'ts of this place than by helping others to navigate them,' Lamine reflects. 'There is no better way to learn than to teach.' Crucially, he could count on a broad pool of 'brothers, uncles and cousins' to support him while he found his feet in Catalonia's vibrant capital. People offered places to stay, invited him to dinner, and showed him where to show up at the crack of dawn to get hired to do small jobs for the day: housework, fieldwork and painting.

He had barely been in the country for six months when, in 2004, one of his 'cousin-friends' named Mbake Kaba rang to offer Lamine a job that he had been doing himself but needed

153

to give up – fixing car exhausts at a company called Thunder Competition. Lamine took the undeclared work without hesitation. He knew this was the kind of job which could eventually lead to obtaining the papers that would allow him to work legally. Lamine worked hard, and his employers were happy with him, even raising his salary. Initially, they remained reluctant to help him get legitimate working papers. Lamine played the situation astutely, offering to leave to save the company trouble. The company responded by asking him to stay – and got him a working permit and an ID card valid for one year. The first year was followed by a second, then a third, and finally, after his fifth year, he qualified as a resident in Spain.

At that point, Lamine heard of yet another West African 'cousin' who had become a cab driver. Lamine enrolled on a course and learned the streets of Barcelona by exploring the entire city, mostly on foot. After three months, he got his licence. After a while, his friend Pablo, with whom he had passed the exam, offered him shared ownership of a taxi, bought a second and asked Lamine to run the small company as well as continuing as a driver. In 2017 Lamine incorporated his own taxi business. He has no immediate plans to expand it and is focused on his family for now.

During his childhood, when business slowed down in Senegal, Lamine's father Salim, a salesman, saw an opportunity to open up shop in Man, an Ivorian town at the crossroads with Liberia and Guinea. He packed the family's belongings in a rented minibus and simply moved the entire family there one day. 'It wasn't like, we've moved to a different country. Just new people and friends. We were technically migrants, but that's not how we felt, and no one saw us as such.' I ask Lamine if his youthful experience of migration influenced his path as a migrant in Spain. 'Of course! In countless ways! In my childhood, I wanted to help my parents, and I immediately realised that our most important priority as traders and as newcomers should be to figure out how to earn people's trust. When you land somewhere where people don't know you, that's the key. Trust is so hard to earn and so easy to lose. I never forgot that. This has been the guiding principle of my life in Spain.'

Growing up in Côte d'Ivoire enriched Lamine's life. 'It was like realising that I was part of a new, bigger club. These days, when I meet people from anywhere around West Africa, but especially from the Ivory Coast, I feel I'm with family. This has allowed me to get help *from* and provide help *to* a whole lot of people since I first arrived in Spain.' It was in Man that Lamine met his wife Fatou, who was his high school sweetheart. Once properly established in Barcelona many years later, Lamine flew her over. They married in 2010 and started a beautiful family.

For Lamine, his dad's decision to migrate and his own have been the most significant shaping forces in his life: 'In Barcelona, I have friends from all over the world. From Senegal, the rest of West Africa and all over Spain, of course. Spaniards from other parts of the country are considered foreigners here,' he adds with a smirk. 'But my friends also come from India and Pakistan, France and Germany. I never stop making new ones. I keep learning about this place, about myself and about humanity. I have been blessed to meet people like Pablo and others, who trusted me, helped me, showed me how things work. I am grateful for what life has given me. I have faith in my fellow man. And I pay my taxes!'

Lamine has never been rich on the global scale, or in the strictest sense. His story is about a different kind of wealth: information, contacts, trust-building and social skills. It's about having someone who will welcome you, put you up and feed you when you land somewhere, who will lend you a phone, possibly vouch for you as you try getting your first job. This explains why many of the countries with the longest, most successful migratory traditions are expert at networking. There are networks of Indians all along the Eastern African coast, all the way to South Africa; the Lebanese of West Africa, traders since their country was known as Phoenicia; Chinese people from the provinces of Fujian; and of course the Irish.

In contrast, rich countries like Japan and the United States, which have extremely small proportions of their populations living abroad, inward-looking mentalities, and a national ethos that tells them that they are better than everyone else, have serious catching up to do, for their own good and that of their young citizens. The world's networking cultures have a head start in the migration revolution at hand. And for this, Lamine has not just his father, but his ancestors to thank.

With this in mind, it's worth reassessing the nature of the refugee. We often talk about helping refugees from a place of simple compassion. I hope it goes without saying that we should be compassionate to refugees, but this compassion, while well-meaning, can be somewhat condescending. The difficulty of the refugee journey, travelling without money into an uncertain future, where, crucially, you don't know anybody, is proof that refugees don't just deserve our sympathy, they deserve our respect. To escape oppression or hunger or war, and seek a new chapter in life, while in part an act of necessity, is also one of optimism. It's an investment in your future, in a belief that it can be better. Lamine told me that he wasn't heroic. Fine – let us say, then, that he is impressive. That someone with Lamine's traumas – impoverished by a brutal civil war, robbed by smugglers – retains his faith in humanity, and is able not only to start again but to thrive, is hugely impressive. Despite trust being easily lost and hard won, Lamine didn't just earn it – he also never stopped trusting others.

This trusting mindset that forges a community is not only on display in today's refugees heading from Africa and the Middle East to Europe. The United States is a nation built not just of immigrants, but of refugees. The earliest settlers included Puritans whose religious views were persecuted in Europe. Waves of refugees followed throughout the generations, seeking to escape persecution, war or famine. Indeed, the Irish community in the US is largely built from those fleeing the crippling famines that hit Ireland in the 1800s.

Modern-day Israel, too, was formed in the aftermath of the Second World War and the Holocaust, and was populated by Jews fleeing the destruction of their homes and the persecution they had suffered under the Nazis. Between 1948 and 1970, 1.15 million Jewish refugees fled to Israel. In 1952, 200,000 of them were living in tent cities, having arrived with nothing. Fast-forward to today, and both the United States and Israel are thriving economies, who have assimilated these refugees into their wider populace successfully. It's not even a question of assimilation – these refugees *are* the wider populace.

The motivations behind a refugee's movement are unique when compared to other migrants, and far more extreme. But the things that they learn on the way, the things that they teach when they arrive in their new home, are all things they have in common with the other migrants we've seen so far in this book. Refugees, by necessity, are expert traders in networks, and, as our world becomes more interconnected than ever before, they have skills that any host country should be thrilled to receive. Being a bad host to asylum seekers is not just a grotesque moral failing; it is also an act of self-sabotage. Refugees such as Lamine add so much to their host countries, that to see them as parasitical, as they are sometimes portrayed in the news media or by populist politicians, is not simply ethically wrong, it is profoundly incorrect to boot. Refugees, whose own communities of origin have been uprooted through no fault of their own, know the value of kinship, and, as Lamine's story expresses, seek to cultivate it wherever they are. In an age of ever-increasing loneliness, and one in which more and more people are on the move than ever before, those who are able to create communities should be honoured citizens wherever they choose to make their homes.

However, this is not to say that the uneasiness people feel about refugees is totally unfounded. There are real reasons for concern. As the world becomes more disordered, as climate change forces greater numbers of people from their homes, greater numbers of refugees are created. Clearly, a country cannot have absolutely no cap and welcome a limitless number of people. There are practical concerns – where will people be housed? Are there enough spaces to educate the children? Do local and social services have enough resources to cope with people? How, and on what basis, do we set limits on the numbers of refugees we accept?

Each country must find its own answer to this question based on their own context, and the purpose of this book isn't to say 'UK: 1 million; France: 1.5 million,' and so on. Rather, it is my intention to portray an ethic of openness here. When considering how and on what basis, Louis Blanc's phrase, often attributed to Karl Marx, 'from each according to their ability, to each according to their needs', seems like a wise rule of thumb. With this in mind, I think that centralised governments often do a terrible job of settling refugees. With numbers concentrated on large metropolises, refugees become ghettoised and isolated. They learn little about the place they have ended up, and have few opportunities to start rebuilding their lives away from the designation 'refugee'. Thoughtfully and sensibly distributed around a nation, however – particularly to places in urgent need of younger people – we can prolong the process of that seamless infusion which has been going for millennia, rather than give rise to fears of an 'invasion'.

From here, the subsequent concerns often voiced regarding refugees start to melt away. For example, many people fear rewarding the criminals who profit from refugees by providing clandestine travel services for them. We see this on our television screens; as dinghies try to cross the Channel between England and France, or the Mediterranean, our ire is targeted on the people traffickers. But the solution is clear. If host nations were not seeking to keep refugees out, refugees would not be forced to make such perilous journeys. The services of people traffickers would not be needed. The gangs are a product of the policies of nations that receive refugees. The best way to eradicate them is first to accept that people are coming, before legislating and organising an infrastructure that suffocates criminal gangs and prevents them profiting from a humanitarian crisis.

What of the risks of terrorists among the refugees? Again, if a nation is prepared to accept refugees, they can start getting ahead of these problems before they emerge. Radicalisation is caused by alienation, and desperation – ensuring that there is a system whereby refugees are properly housed, fed, placed into welcoming communities and given decent jobs will do more to protect people than ever more stringent security procedures. It should also be remembered that the majority of terrorist attacks conducted in the name of an insane interpretation of Islam in Europe have been perpetrated by those radicalised in Europe, not foreigners coming to Europe. What holds for refugees holds for them, too – societies without alienated, desperate people do not produce terrorists.

The same can be said of health concerns, which are largely overblown to start with. TB and coronavirus are a danger if they go undetected. Having a system in place that allows people to seek asylum easily means that illnesses can be screened for. The real danger occurs when, due to the difficulty posed by crossing borders, refugees sneak in with health problems, work in undocumented positions and are, by and large, invisible to health professionals and epidemiologists. Being accepting of refugees, and seeking to care for them, means that you can screen them and keep the wider populace safe, too.

•◆•

Perhaps, for personal reasons, the sense of community that Lamine talked about in the previous chapter resonates especially strongly with me. A community can have reasonably loose links – like the community of 'cousins' Lamine relied upon when he was first in Spain – but as long as there is some thread that weaves a sense of togetherness between them, it is hard to break the bond of fellowship.

I know this because each and every day, I make at least four phone calls to other alcoholics and addicts in recovery spread out around the world. I call Greece, India, East Africa, Australia, New Zealand and Hawaii in the morning, France, London or Germany around lunchtime and the continental US from 3pm onwards. Once a week, a group of us from every continent have a phone meeting. We talk about our recovery, about how we are doing, what's on our mind, our problems, our joys, our fears and our hopes. The sense of being connected, the peace of mind and serenity it brings, are priceless.

As I travel, even when I find myself in a city or country where I don't know anyone, most of the time I can go online and find a venue nearby where I can sit with perfect strangers in a circle and share unconditional support and love. I have done so in the Bronx and Tokyo, in Senegal and Malaysia, in Kansas and Brandenburg, Dubai and Las Vegas, Greece and Australia. Being a proud member of this community allows me to feel safe wherever I go. When I first moved to Sweden in the dead of winter, it enabled me to overcome the paralysing waves of loneliness I felt and provided the psychological and spiritual support I needed until I found my bearings.

Friends in recovery welcome me into their homes and put me up on their couches. They feed me and, crucially, listen to me when I feel low. And I have the good fortune of doing the same for others and, in so doing, of partaking in the magic virtuous circle of selfish selflessness that keeps us sober and clean. When I look back at where I come from as an alcoholic and addict – at the pain caused, the damage and the wreckage of my past – and I look at the miracle of my life in recovery, I see this ever-present potential for connection as one of the greatest privileges and indeed one of the most beautiful things in my life.

Not everyone is an addict. But everyone is something. And you only need one thing to form a community with others. Whether you are into video games or football, Japanese aquarelles or Chilean wine, Vipassana meditation or opera, hip-hop or tango, Scrabble or chess, dark matter or dinosaurs (or both), there is something about you that can spark a network. The point is, you don't need an existing network to get started. All you need in this day and age is a passion – or a problem, in my case – or even just an interest in something, anything, to initiate contact with people who down the line might provide a base for you to get started – wherever it is you hope to go.

The importance of the network for the migrant is heavily impacted by and has far-reaching consequences for an era of constant change in the way we communicate and network. Social media can be incredibly detrimental to our well-being when used addictively, triggering an unhealthy dependence on the opinion of others while building advertising revenue for entities who arguably should be the ones paying for our personal data. But social media has incredible value when it is used as a means to initiate real, offline connections. In truth, these technologies arguably represent the single most important development of our age for the New Nomad. Fossil-fuel intensive travel is likely (hopefully) going to be heavily impacted by global carbon taxes as we belatedly come to terms with the aberrant cost of and damage caused by our high-entropy, energy-intensive civilisation. Information-intensive technologies are likely to have a rosier future.

For instance, the Venezuelan exodus since 2015, one of the swiftest and largest in Latin American history, has led to the emergence of groups on social media like *Venezolanos en la Argentina* and *Venezolanos en Madrid*, which allow aspiring Venezuelan migrants to find and support each other easily.

But new technologies are also allowing us to find each other according to other affiliations. Older networks – religious, national and ethnic networks linking members of diasporas with each other and with the homeland – still carry a lot of weight, but what characterises our time is the speed and ease with which the New Nomad can tap into new networks, and the speed and ease with which those networks can emerge and evolve.

·•·

In the early hours of 27 January 2014, the forces of the Clusterfuck Coalition and Russian Alliances got ready to launch their attack. The epic battle against N3 and Pandemic Legion, which would come to be known as the Bloodbath of B-R5RB, was about to begin. It would prove to be a decisive turn in the Halloween War, would last twenty-one hours and involve 7,500 people from around the world.

If you haven't heard of this battle, it's probably because you're not into EVE Online, one of the oldest and most renowned role-playing video games of all time. According to Wikipedia, EVE is a 'space-based, persistent world massively multiplayer online role-playing game'. In more mundane terms, it is an incredibly vast and complex universe in terms of player interactions (the game contains a total of 7,800 star systems that can be visited by players, of whom there are hundreds of thousands). One crucial component of the EVE Online magic has to do with the fact that entropy, the second law of thermodynamics, holds in the game – one can't undo what has been done or happened in the EVE universe, which

164

includes unscripted economic competition, warfare and political schemes with other players.

Once a year, the EVE *Fanfest* gathers thousands of the game's participants in Reykjavik. Players hail from very different places, cultures and backgrounds. EVE Online players have been known to finance each other's trips to Iceland, with teams pooling money together to pay for the journey and stay of less affluent members in Iceland's famously expensive hotels, and making complex schedules so everyone on a team, and sometimes entire federations, can meet up for dinner.

Brynar Emilsson is eighteen years old and works at a food stand in Reykjavik, selling hot dogs. He has been playing another multiplayer game called *World of Warcraft* since he was five years old. In the fantasy game – these games are all online descendants of the role-playing game Dungeons & Dragons, which many nerds of my generation, including myself, were into – his avatar was named Etlasafi. At some point, Etlasafi encountered another character in the game named Crimson. The two were so passionate about the game that, like players around the world, they were willing to shell out $15 a month in subscription fees to kill orcs and goblins together. Before long they knew quite a lot about each other, and so, in 2014, when Brynar went to Bulgaria on holiday, he swung by the mall where his friend worked and the two hung out, turning a virtual friendship into a reality. The entire premise of that encounter, an Icelandic adolescent becoming friends with a Bulgarian one by teaming up virtually in a video game, leading to a real-life meeting, was unthinkable just a few years ago. This unprecedented way of making connections has far-reaching consequences not only for individuals or education, but also for our politics.

During the course of their lives and as they travel the world, the new nomads may join new tribes. This is not a novel aberration but a deeply entrenched human habit. Yet this fluidity doesn't ring true to many people, who feel some forms of kinship (national, religious and ethnic allegiances) ought to outweigh all others. Their argument goes something like this: imagine that you are a Welshwoman who loves Nigerian literature. It wouldn't influence your life choices. You wouldn't seek out a Nigerian literature-loving companion in the same way that people like Aaron, the Trump supporter in Montana, seek co-religionists to marry. In the same spirit, if you were a motorcyclist, you might feel a kinship with bikers around the world. But that would never trump your national allegiance.

But for the new nomads, national solidarity might well be trumped by more niche identities. It is likely, for instance, that the people behind Etlasafi and Crimson have more in common with each other than they do with their fellow Icelanders and Bulgarians. Though an embrace of such networks doesn't translate into a rejection of their roots or their tribes, the bond and solidarity between EVE Online players extends well beyond what happens around the annual gathering. EVE Online players are known to have helped other players get new jobs, and arrange insurance cover for their houses. Some have married and had children together.

The transnational and translocal climate networks which

are both locally grounded and infused with a global ethos and a shared sense of belonging are natural homes for the new nomads: because they learn and thrive on connection, all migrants, from relatively privileged digital nomads, whom we'll meet shortly, to refugees from poor countries, have more in common than we tend to think. Many thrive on connection and seamlessly become expert connectors. We can see in Brynar something of Lamine and vice versa. Connection with peers, and a lack thereof, is the fundamental difference between a fearful, angry refugee and one who flourishes.

This is where Western countries fail. When refugees arrive, they may well have had experiences that make them less affable than Lamine. They may be traumatised, vulnerable or unable to control their emotions adequately. But, as I have experienced in my own struggles with addiction and mentioned in the introduction to this book, there can be post-traumatic growth as well as post-traumatic stress. To be clear, I am in no way equating my experiences to those of a refugee. What I am saying is that, for addicts certainly, a supportive community is the number one thing to expedite recovery.

It holds that there is a parallel truth in the experience of refugees, too. Beyond the essentials of life like shelter and food – which may be grudgingly given – refugees also need to be offered a community. Too often, though, the bureaucratic processes that surround asylum claims isolate them. These processes can separate them from other refugees and, perhaps more importantly, from the host population. Upon arrival, we should be doing everything we can to

167

kickstart the refugee's ability to start building a network and become part of a community – and in this digital age, as shown by the EVE Online example, it is easier than ever to meet somebody who shares an interest of yours in real life. Unfortunately, however, a set of policies adopted in many countries, from Britain's Hostile Environment to the United States' border internment camps, frustrates refugees' ability to build community.

Beyond the moral failure this represents, it is an astonishing squandering of human potential. Othering is at the heart of this wastage. By labelling refugees as just one thing, and treating them (badly) accordingly, we limit their ability to flourish. How can we move beyond labels?

7

THE LIMITS OF LABELS

'Definitions belong to the definers, not the defined.'

Toni Morrison, *Beloved*

In December 2018, a young student of architecture in Lyon was flown to Tokyo by Turkish Airlines, who treated him to a business-class journey in return for posting videos about his experience. His YouTube comedy channel, which at the time of writing boasts almost three million followers, proved an attractive audience for the airline. But Amr Maskoun isn't your typical YouTuber. You could hardly tell from listening to him speak – his French is stellar – but Amr is a Syrian refugee.

When I first met Amr and his older brother Shahm, I was writing in a village not far from Lyon. They came and stayed over for a weekend. I was immediately struck by the manners and earnestness of the two brothers, and by how different they seemed. Shahm is sturdy, manly and opinionated. He is well but soberly dressed. Amr, on the other hand, is thin, shy, androgynous and something of a fashionista. He is very quiet at first, but he comes alive once you get him talking. When he starts impersonating people, he's hilarious. I can easily imagine him on stage doing stand-up comedy.

Shahm, the firstborn, was the family pioneer who made it to France and managed to reunite the entire family there. He had since become more of a father figure than a brother to Amr. He now worked in Paris as a telecoms engineer for Huawei Technologies. It was he who chose the quieter city of Lyon for the family to settle down in and go local.

Like most Syrians of their age, the two brothers have been through a lot, though they're well aware that they are among the luckiest Syrian expatriates. Amr was twelve when he left Syria. When war broke out in the south of the country, people in Aleppo thought the conflict would never reach them. Shahm was studying engineering in the south and took part in peaceful protests only to be arrested and tortured. When he was released, he skipped town. Soon enough, soldiers started showing up unannounced looking for Shahm (to force him into their ranks), barging into the family home, shouting and eyeing the boys' sister Ghazwa in an insistent, threatening way. That was enough for Wahid, their father, to send the family to Turkey. They expected to return 'as soon as the fighting blew over', but it never did.

The family had been well-off before the war, living in a comfortable apartment in an upper-class neighbourhood in the heart of town. Lama, the mother, is of patrician descent and has a degree in literary Arabic. When they'd first met, she hadn't been too keen on Wahid, who didn't go to university. Wahid's family was poor. He started out as a street vendor but went on to build a thriving import/export business. When war came, Amr had just taken an important set of exams and, like other teenagers, he thought mostly about school and friends. After Wahid sent the family out of Syria, they roamed between Turkey, Lebanon and the United Arab Emirates for a year in search of a place where Amr could attend high school. In 2013, he and his mother and sister settled in Turkey, where they had permission to stay for a year at a time. Amr went to a Turkish school in Ankara for a year, then spent the next four years in an Arabic school in Istanbul, graduating with honours.

In Istanbul, Shahm, and Amr's other brother Nador, spent months sleeping on park benches at night and guiding tourists by day. By the time Lama, Ghazwa and Amr made it to Turkey, the pair had reached France, where they were granted permanent refugee status. Amr sank into a deep depression with his sister and mother in Ankarra, spending most of his time locked up in his room, refusing to learn Turkish because he resented the way Syrians were treated in Turkey. Eventually, Shahm and Nador saved enough money to buy Amr an iPad, and he started learning other languages by watching videos on YouTube and repeating the sounds.

The family lived in constant fear that Wahid, like so many Syrians, would be killed by the regime. Amr, who had always been the family clown, decided he had to try to make them smile. As news of the massacres of neighbours, relatives

171

and friends kept coming, this was no trivial matter. The family's mental health depended on it. He started to shoot short comedy videos of himself. His first effort explored the troubles of 'Susan', a teenaged girl who had to do the dishes during Ramadan, when extended families and friends gather at the end of the day's fast to devour huge dinners. I've watched it with him, while he translated since I hardly speak Arabic, and found it hilarious. His friends and family loved it. He made more videos in a similar vein.

One day he posted one on Facebook without giving it much thought, went out with friends and returned a few hours later to find it had gone viral. Susan's mother was known as Umm Susan – the name is a feminist dig at the way Arab women are known as the mothers of their sons rather than as themselves. His impression of Susan and her family made Amr one of the Arab world's most-followed YouTubers. He played every other member of her family, too: the absent father and husband, the brother, and her precocious little devil of a sister. Before long, Amr was a social media star.

Three years on, Amr was living in France, where the family has been reunited, and, besides his mother tongue, spoke French like a Lyonnais and English very fluently. He was still busy trying to integrate himself into French society and to get to understand what makes the French laugh. Amr was passionate about languages and was still learning new ones (Italian, when we spoke). He starts with sounds. Then he memorises vocabulary and practices speaking with others. 'If we start with grammar, as the French do, we will learn nothing. No wonder no one in this country can speak

English to save their lives. Who writes in a language they can't speak?'

Amr believes that humour connects people and can be a powerful tool for peace. Laughing together is about connection. Humour is one of the most natural ways a traveller connects with those he meets. When you are laughing with someone, you cannot be Othering them, too.

Amr possessed many of the qualities that millennials are said to lack: he was deeply moral, humble and keen to learn; he was reserved but proud to be a refugee. When I asked him how he felt about it, he literally jumped up: 'I'm not just proud. I'm deeply grateful that I'm a refugee! Not just because we are among the lucky survivors. Growing up in Syria, Turkey and France has been an incredible privilege. Whatever God sends my way, I know deep down I can handle it. Being a migrant has allowed me to learn and open my mind.'

So is Amr Maskoun a Syrian refugee, a migrant or a successful Arab YouTuber?

Putting labels on people – refugee, migrant, expat – causes us to oversimplify what are actually complex situations. For every Amr, of course, there are thousands of other young Syrian refugees with less fortunate experiences. Each story is unique in its own way. What is really important is to look at the character and personality of the people we are talking about, not the label we put on them. Amr's story of safe passage and flourishing abroad doesn't have to be exceptional.

•◆•

Following on from our discussion about refugees and networks, in this chapter we will consider the increasing conflation of the words 'migrant' (which is supposed to apply to anyone living one year or more in a country other than their country of birth) and 'refugee' in everyday conversation. Similarly, we pigeonhole migrants into groups depending on where they come from and where they are going, what colour their skin is, and how poor (or wealthy) they are.

Of course, it's important to make a distinction between migration by choice and migration out of necessity. The former is a manifestation of social mobility, a freedom *to*; the latter an issue of social justice, of freedom *from*.

There are excellent reasons for using certain terms for specific kinds of migrants, chief among them that they enable us to identify those most in need of protection. In his book *Refuge*, co-authored with Alexander Betts, the Oxford economist Paul Collier explains why we came up with the term 'refugees' and why we differentiate them from other migrants. Refugees, he explains, are *forced* to migrate by war, famine, natural disaster or persecution: they are seeking refuge. This puts them in a different category to people who *choose* to migrate. As Mikael Ribbenvik, the head of the Swedish Migration Agency, pointed out to me, this distinction is crucial to ensure that people fleeing political persecution, war or genocide are afforded special treatment by countries who are adopting increasingly strict immigration policies.

But this healthy distinction leads to an unhealthy double standard: immigrants are often painted as invasive and/or miserable folk coming 'over here' to burden our societies, while emigration is broadly portrayed as a project reserved for the wealthy. One rule for 'us' and another for 'them'. In truth, almost all migration has a personal, a political and a social element.

This chapter will show how breaking down the labels that we put on people better allows us to respect them for who they are, and not where they come from, or why.

•◆•

For several years, I worked for the government of Georgia as a kind of private diplomat/connector and media relations advisor. One of my jobs was bringing over opinion-makers from Europe and the United States to give them a sense of this remarkable little country. Until they saw it with their own eyes, most of them thought Georgia was no more than a collection of images of Russian troops roaming the countryside and run-down villages, Chechnya-style. By the time they left, they knew about the country's colourful, proud and generous people, its renowned cuisine, its surreal diversity of climates, its location at the crossroads of Islam and Christianity, its strikingly beautiful ancient alphabet, and its bold (some would say rash) reformist political leadership. Working for the Georgians was how I met Vera Kobalia.

In 1992, when Vera was eleven years old, war broke out in her native Abkhazia, a particularly stunning region of Georgia, as a result of the collapse of the Soviet Union. It opposed the country's newly independent government and Abkhaz separatist forces backed by Russia, in a rehearsal of what happened in 2008 when Russian tanks reinvaded the region and convinced Venezuela, Nicaragua, Nauru and Syria to recognise it as an independent state (that in turn seems to have served as a trial run for Russia's invasion of Ukraine in 2014, and Abkhazia remains occupied to this day).

Soon after the war started, looting became rife, and one night soldiers came to Vera's house to rob the family. The next morning they fled to Tbilisi, the Georgian capital, where they stayed for a year before moving to Moscow. With his logical mind, her father, a mathematics professor, reinvented himself as a successful businessman, but organised crime in Moscow soon made life dangerous. Under increasing pressure from extortionists, he applied for permanent residency in Canada. After two years, the family was accepted and offered a choice of city. They went to a bookstore that had just one book about Canada – a tourist guide to Vancouver. They knew little else of Canada, so Vancouver was where they went.

They did remarkably well starting their lives over from scratch, in a new world, with a new language and new rules. Within a few years, Vera's mother was working in IT, Vera's father had built a successful vegan bakery business, and Vera herself, now armed with a business degree, worked for him. As a flourishing young Georgian businesswoman abroad, she caught the attention of government officials back home. When Georgia's president, Mikheil Saakashvili, visited the Canadian Parliament during the 2010 Winter Olympics, he mentioned her by name in his speech as an example of a successful Georgian émigré. Vera returned to Georgia and co-founded an NGO to help displaced Abkhazians. She was soon a recognisable public figure in the small country. At the age of just twenty-eight, she was appointed Minister of the Economy and Sustainable Development.

I remember hosting dinners in Paris and Tbilisi with her and 'Misha', as Georgians called Saakashvili. Vera and I travelled together to Silicon Valley and had meetings with companies like Tesla and Google, and the mayor of San Francisco. Everywhere, Vera lit up the room. People could barely hide their surprise that this beautiful young woman was a leading figure in a government. As a minister, she cut through red tape, and the country went from 141st to 11th in the World Bank's ranking for ease of doing business. It wasn't a gentle process, though. The fight against corruption was accompanied by Thatcher-inspired reforms which proved bruising for many Georgians, who in 2012 voted Saakashvili out of power.

Hardly skipping a beat, Vera moved on to advise other countries. She tried working for the Kazakh government, despite her reservations about the one-party state. It didn't last. 'After four or five months, we were done. They kept telling me my ideas were too revolutionary. I didn't want to find myself behind bars.' After that, she advised more benign governments in Eastern Europe. Then, in 2015, she moved to Jakarta to advise Indonesia's Minister of Trade as well as President Joko Widodo's chief of staff.

Meanwhile, her six-year-old daughter Anastasia had become 'the real nomad' of the family. Nicknamed Nino, as is common for the countless Anastasias of Georgia, she has been on the road since birth and doesn't know any other way. It's part of her life, and she has friends everywhere. In Jakarta, the little Georgian girl was learning Mandarin in an Australian kindergarten. The last time the family visited Singapore, Vera and her husband were in a cab speaking Georgian to each other and English to their daughter, and Nino started singing a song in Mandarin. Singapore is one of the most ethnically diverse places in the world, and local cab drivers are usually unfazed by this kind of stuff. But this one literally stopped the car, Vera remembers vividly. 'Where on earth are you from?! Your daughter speaks better Mandarin than my kids, and I'm Chinese!'

After a stint in Hong Kong in 2018, during which Vera taught at the Asia Global Institute, in 2019 the family made its way back to Vancouver, where Vera sits on the Economic Development Board for New Westminster and the board of several of Canadian companies. She has one main message for aspiring young nomads. Her life has taken her from rural Abkhazia to Vancouver as a refugee. She came back to Georgia and now back to Canada as a successful Canadian: 'If it were not for forced migration, my parents would have been in the same jobs and the same place for the rest of their lives, and my life would have been radically different. I am grateful we travelled to the other side of the world. I am who I am because we were forced to move.'

However unsettling it might seem to talk about refugees in this way, for Vera there is something inherently *good* about migrating, regardless of circumstances. It is possible that all of the great benefits of migration highlighted in the previous chapters are available to every migrant, irrespective of the reasons for their migration. Or at least, it could be possible if refugees were not treated as categorically different types of people.

•◆•

Mustafa Al Sarajj was huddled together with his colleagues at the back of the store when the manager walked in with a sombre look. The staff had been chatting amiably. That gave way to a nervous silence. The owner of the store, Sven Larsson, a middle-aged man with severe eyebrows, braced himself for what he had to say. He had called this emergency meeting of his thirteen staff. Some were still in their red and green 7-Eleven uniforms, having just finished their shift. Others had come in on their day off. The manager took a deep breath and, in precise, dead-pan Swedish, explained the problem. 'The figures don't add up, guys,' he said. 'I've checked and double-checked. There is only one conclusion – somebody is stealing money.' The small crowd shuffled listlessly. Then, one by one, twelve heads turned to stare accusingly at the young man standing shyly in the corner. Since he was one of the few who weren't stealing, the other employees had conspired to turn on him.

In contrast to Vera's welcome to Canada, Mustafa didn't have it easy when he first landed in Sweden. He was born in Damascus, Syria, to two Iraqi immigrants who had fled Saddam Hussein's brutal regime. He arrived in Stockholm at the age of twenty-three as a refugee, with no friends, no money, no knowledge of Swedish and nowhere to stay. He slept in an internet café for a few nights, trawling online forums in search of somebody who would host a penniless migrant. Sweden being Sweden, he eventually found a kind spirit online who was willing to put him up while he looked for work.

He found a job at a 7-Eleven in central Stockholm and started studying economics at university in Swedish and English. He could now afford food and rent, but between work and his studies had little spare time. 'My life was a never-ending cycle of work, study, work, study. I would take all the double shifts I could because I needed the cash. My commute was two and a half hours in total, so my manager let me sleep on the floor in the back storeroom, working eighteen hours straight. It was hard work, and I was constantly exhausted, but it was exactly what I needed at the time. Exactly zero time to think about my situation and feel sorry for myself.'

Mustafa had been working as the manager of three different 7-Elevens for six months when his boss held the fateful emergency staff meeting. Sven had thought of Mustafa as one of his best employees. He dismissed everyone and took Mustafa aside. 'Why did you do this, Mustafa? I gave you a job, I promoted you, I gave you extra shifts and let you sleep here when you needed.'

When the tirade was over, Mustafa simply pulled a worn notebook from his uniform pocket and handed it to his manager. Inside was a list of dates and times, a record of occasions when he had spotted his colleagues stealing from the till. His boss corroborated them against the security cameras to see for himself who was really stealing. Mustafa recalled, 'He was livid. He told me later that he had never felt so ashamed.' Though Mustafa initially walked away, angry and hurt, and refused to answer calls from him, his former boss didn't relent and, after months of efforts, managed to track him down through another employee. He came to his doorstep, apologising profusely and even breaking down in tears. Mustafa agreed to come back to work for him.

Sven went further to say sorry. Before long, he suggested Mustafa become his own boss and buy a 7-Eleven franchise in Stockholm's hipster paradise Södermalm, putting him in touch with the relevant contacts and recommending him to colleagues. Even without the burden of rent arrears, Mustafa struggled to get together the necessary funds to buy the new store. The bank rejected his application for credit, but his reputation as a straight arrow allowed him to pull together the funds by borrowing money from Sven and friends. He moved into his store the week he bought it. It was in a filthy state, infested with rats and cockroaches, but he cleaned it up and turned it into a gem. When Sven retired, he sold Mustafa a second franchise, the best one in Stockholm.

With careful management, he managed to accumulate more premises, and before long, he owned eight different 7-Eleven franchises. 'When Sven helped me get that first store, I knew it was my chance, and I took it. I worked hard, harder than I've ever worked in my entire life. I was there from opening to closing every day. But the money rolled in.'

After his second child was born, Mustafa decided to sell off most of his stores in order to spend more time with his wife Zeyneb and the children. 'I realised that I was missing the best years of my children's lives. My daughter was five years old, and I had hardly spent any time with her. I had never done any of the normal things that fathers do with their children, especially here in Sweden. Something needed to change.' And so Mustafa became an Uber driver so he could work around his wife and children's schedule and have a family life. That didn't last. In less than six months, he was noticed by the company for having the best ratings of all the drivers in Stockholm and was swiftly offered a corporate job. He is now team leader, in charge of the training pro-grammes for drivers throughout the whole of Scandinavia.

Dividing people into YouTubers, like Amr, expats, like Vera, or refugees, like Mustafa, makes little sense. Amr and Vera are also refugees; Mustafa is also an executive at Uber. Of course, these are particularly successful refugees. But that's precisely the point. Hastily applied labels can per-petuate stereotypes about how different we are, instead of allowing us to focus on what we have in common. A label can become a self-fulfilling prophecy. Different types of migrants are not different types of human beings. And while the personal, political and social stimuli for their rationale for migrating differ, their stories show that yesterday's refugee can become something else, often anything else, tomorrow.

It's important to re-state this because, clearly, we live in a time when what Vera sees as the inherent good of migration is fundamentally contested. To start trying to understand why migration is getting a bad rap, we're going to look at the most mobile new migrant of all – the digital nomad.

8

RISE AND FALL OF THE 'DIGITAL NOMAD'

On a Thursday afternoon in the spring of 2018, a group of twenty- and thirty-somethings gathered in the function room of a coworking space in central London. In one corner stood a makeshift bar where a bartender handed out free bottles of IPA from a local microbrewery. 'What's a microbrewery?' one attendee asked. A bearded man laughed. The attendees stood around in twos and threes conversing in a brand of Commonwealth or American English, or the more tentative, global variety. The vibe was casual – most people were dressed in sneakers and T-shirts, but a few wore blazers.

Few outsiders would consider having beers on a Thursday afternoon at work. But, for those present, events like this were clearly a regular part of their professional lives. The event was a gathering of 'digital nomads', people who wander the globe doing all their work remotely using laptop computers. They have no permanent bosses, no permanent office, few commitments and the freedom to work whenever and wherever they like. 'It's a travel junkie's dream,' one attendee submitted, pensively. Events like this are where they build connections and, in many cases, meet their colleagues for the first time. Some of the attendees had been chatting online for years without having actually met face to face. 'He looks different to his Slack photo,' one mentioned jokingly. The person in question blushed.

Prior to the coronavirus, remote working was already becoming increasingly feasible for increasing numbers of people, and a new class of global worker had emerged. As I write this in the summer of 2020, during the midst of the pandemic, remote working has expanded exponentially, becoming a necessity to millions of workers. As with many things, the pandemic served to accelerate a trend that was already nascent: the location of an office matters less now than it did in the pre-internet age. For those lucky enough to be in an 'office job', there is no need for an 'office' at all.

At first glance, it's an enormously attractive idea, particularly for the young. You get to travel, potentially indefinitely, and do your work on your own terms. With internet connectivity spreading throughout the world, even to quite rural and remote areas, plausibly you can work from anywhere. No fixed hours, no humdrum routine, nobody telling you what to do. A quick search of the term 'digital nomad' will present you with lots of toothy young people extolling the virtues of working from a beach in Thailand, which, it has to be said, does sound significantly more pleasant than working in an office in Slough. I should point out here; I totally understand the joys associated with this lifestyle. As I hope this book is making clear, I love to travel. I think it's important.

I strongly believe in the positive power of migration. I also like sitting on the beach (though not for too long) – I'm not made of stone. Indeed, I was, for many years, a kind of digital nomad myself.

Digital nomads are, inevitably, less fixed to the country of their birth. Most of them come from countries that are associated with wealth and status in our northern-gone-global consciousness. Few come from the (mostly Muslim) countries which issue green-coloured passports. There are for example very few Pakistani digital nomads because those passports will not allow for visa-free travel to many other countries. It perhaps comes as no surprise that other forms of privilege are essentials to be packed into the overhead compartment, too. Digital nomads tend to come from wealthy countries, and tend to be from wealthy backgrounds within those countries. The clue is in the 'digital' – these workers tend to be highly skilled and part of the knowledge economy. Though it might be technically possible, there are no YouTube channels promoting the benefits of moving around the world working from a factory in China one day, and one in Brazil the next.

During the coronavirus pandemic, a new kind of passport privilege has emerged. For most of 2020, as a US citizen, it was very hard to travel out of the country. But if you were a dual citizen, you could simply use your other passport to get out, which had many Americans scrambling to try to get a different passport based on foreign ancestry (countries like Ireland with rich histories of migration to the US actually suspended the process which allowed Americans to use their Irish heritage to claim citizenship). This isn't only an

American phenomenon, either. Think about it. Wherever you are in the world, it's almost impossible to stop someone holding a passport from a different country from leaving. In the age of Covid-19, dual citizenship means freedom.

Typical digital nomad jobs might include graphic designers, programmers and writers. But really anything that can be done remotely can be a profession for a digital nomad. Indeed, the range of businesses at the coworking space in central London was as varied as the accents. Some wrote personal travel blogs (in fact a disproportionate number of them did). Travel blogging is the Ponzi scheme of digital nomadism: 'Pay for my travels by reading/watching me give advice on how you can get paid for your travels.'

Others ran sophisticated business outfits like digital creative and advertising agencies, with remote workers spread across dozens of countries. Some were stopping over on their way to visit family in the Midlands. One was en route to Northern Ireland. Many were in London for projects they ran. Others were heading off to more affordable parts of the world: already clichéd digital nomad hotspots like Chiang Mai in Thailand, Kigali, the capital of Rwanda, or Medellín in Colombia, where the cost of living is comparatively low and, as a result, for these aristocrats of contemporary nomadism, the quality of life is high. Their usual *modus operandi* is to stay for a few months, establish a set of local friends (some of them keepers, to be sure) and preferred local cafés, before flying off to some other big city like New York, Tokyo or Berlin and starting the whole process again.

In that room, I doubt that anybody was thinking of

Tuaregs or our hunter-gatherer ancestors when the term 'nomad' came up. Instead, more and more, these young people who identify themselves as nomadic mean something innately twenty-first century. Modernity and its obsession with high-speed mobility has turned nomadism, like so many other things, on its head. Nomadism in Europe in the mid-twentieth century was about homelessness and undesirable and unwelcome vagrancy.

In the early twenty-first century, alongside those young people with their laptops on exotic beaches, it's easy to find endless quotes from celebrities and socialites seemingly convinced that a strict regimen of first-class travel and five-star palaces somehow qualifies as nomadism. And indeed, those are two fundamental stages of life as fantasised by Silicon Valley (and, by extension, the world): learn to code and become a digital nomad, create a start-up, become immensely rich and accede to the lifestyle of a proper global nomad, a full-time traveller who wanders the world of their own accord without a fixed abode, place of employment, or localised circle of friends. One of the most powerful realisations I had while writing this book came during my last visit to the World Economic Forum in Davos, when it occurred to me that there probably wasn't a single place in the world where the concept of nomadism was more popular.

The Economist started running special reports in the 2000s on this new breed of young businesspeople trotting around the globe with their BlackBerrys (how quaint) and laptops in hand. At the time it seemed the novel result of an era increasingly characterised by the ability to move around. But the

187

idea has far earlier antecedents. In the 1980s, Jacques Attali, an economist advising French President François Mitterrand, used the term 'hyper-nomad' to describe a new way of thinking of the elite at a time when mobility had become the best measure of privilege.

When I worked for the *International Herald Tribune* from 2004 to 2006, I was a technologically challenged version of this new breed of nomads. I travelled back and forth constantly between London, where the paper's marketing department was based, and Paris, where its newsroom had been since the publication was founded as the European edition of the *New York Herald* in 1887. To my utter delight, CNN asked to interview me for a segment on 'the rise of the super-commuter'.

I recently dug up the text version of the piece that came out of this interview, and the kindest thing I can say about it is that I wasn't at my smartest or most self-aware. At one point I remarked that 'taking the train from Paris to London feels like hopping on the Tube to go to work'. Looking back, I find the way I expressed how pleased I was with myself embarrassing, but not, I think, unique, coming from a young professional in an age where rapid mobility is the ultimate status symbol, and international mobility the ultimate mark of privilege. What CNN was telling me was that I was one of the 'winners'.

As I started advising governments and multinationals in the ensuing years, increasingly frenzied global travel went hand in hand with increasingly frenzied self-regard. My Instagram account became an example of the kind of techno-narcissism that has become the hallmark of our age, a meaningless stream of pictures, styled as though random but actually carefully curated, featuring, well, me. Me with the famous and the powerful (Sarkozy, Clinton, Gates) or just *me, me, me* in as many places as possible in rapid succession, ideally in front of recognisable landmarks or, if none were available, in a random plane cabin with the location feature turned on. Me in front of the Acropolis on Monday, the Hong Kong skyline Thursday and Christ the Redeemer in Rio at the weekend. Me riding camelback, on a ski lift, a plane, a train, the beach, in the forest, on an elephant or hugging a baby orangutan.

I felt I was entitled to this life, and didn't even attempt to grapple with the fact that my hyper-mobility hinged on the lack of mobility of almost everyone else. That's not to even begin talking about my complete lack of awareness of the environmental cost of high-speed mobility. Nevertheless, chastened though I feel now, I was a pioneer in what has to be one of the most appalling fads of the past decades, which is likely to be among the few victims of the pandemic no one will mourn: competitive travel.

This life started for me back in the mid-2000s, and it was still reasonably novel. Today, there are thousands of articles, blogs and social media posts attesting to the luxury of the digital nomad's lifestyle and luring young people to join an endless spring break parade of beers and beaches. It is easy to see in all of this digital flotsam and jetsam a certain amount of self-satisfaction, and it's very easy to understand why it irritates. There is a sense that the underlying message is, 'I'm so talented I can do my job wherever, and therefore I hang out in great places, making lots of money, while you're tied to your desk.'

Yet, of course, the circumstances of digital nomads fundamentally differ from lots of other migrants who not only struggle and work hard to achieve but partake of their new communities and often give back to their old ones. They also differ from people who are unable to migrate. If you do not have the right passport or the right education, or you have people who depend on you, you cannot do as those fluff pieces in the weekend papers recommend and 'follow your dreams'. And it is extremely annoying to be told that you should.

Nevertheless, a growing number of young people are tempted by this lifestyle. Gonzalo certainly was.

Gonzalo Sanchez Sarmiento was born and raised in Córdoba, Argentina. He started a degree in economics at a local university but dropped out to join the marketing team of a tech firm based in Cincinnati, Ohio, which he had identified, approached and offered his services to, all from his laptop. This was less about earning money and more about gaining an education. This *was* an education. Gonzalo knew that he would be far more employable on the global job market with that experience than with a random Argentinian university degree. He moved back to Argentina and worked as a remote freelancer using his US contacts to find work. That gave way to proper digital nomadism.

By the time we met in the summer of 2018 in Paris, where he was then living, Gonzalo had been working remotely for five years, using his flexible lifestyle to live in New York, Chicago, Tokyo, Stockholm, Malta, Singapore, Hong Kong, Barcelona, Punta del Este and Santiago de Chile. Not only had he been able to live in all these places, but he had also made a good living. With the value of the currency plummeting and rampant inflation, most Argentinians had been struggling to find work, let alone make a decent living, for a decade. Gonzalo had so much on that he had to start turning work down. He estimated that even if he could find a similar job back home, he would only be paid about 20 per cent of what he got paid working remotely.

When we met in Paris, he was working as a software engineer for Jobbatical, a start-up that helps businesses hire staff from around the world and relocate them. Jobbatical was led by a charismatic Estonian, Karoli Hindriks, who was an enthusiastic graduate of Singularity University, the brainchild of the world's most famous techno-utopian author: Ray Kurzweil. When I had visited her at the company headquarters in Tallinn a few months earlier, they felt and smelled and looked like a miniature version of the offices of Google that I visited in Mountain View, New York and Paris. The company and the service it provided were one and the same. The atmosphere had a distinct, post-national, techno-enthusiast feel to it. The employees, hailing from Egypt, New Mexico or Singapore, were your typical Jobbatical users. The company's website was geared mainly to cater to aspiring digital nomads (following a B to C, or Business to Consumer, model). Since then, the messaging has become somewhat more corporate, the company rebranded as 'the efficient, reliable immigration partner for hyper-growth start-ups and global companies'.

Digital nomadism has become a big business. Since its early days in the 2000s, hundreds of thousands of travel-hungry youths have left their nine-to-five jobs behind – if they ever had one in the first place – to partake in this appealing, adventurous and often lucrative lifestyle. Jobbatical's niche has become quite crowded. Today there is a whole industry of conferences, online courses and publications surrounding the lifestyle. The promise boils down to a simple, enticing proposition: 'Get paid to travel the world.'

Yet as we talked at the bar of a café in the Latin Quarter over croissants, I got the sense that something was off for Gonzalo. As we sipped (coffee for him, chocolate milk for me), he gave me his honest take on the digital nomad experience.

The problem had nothing to do with working for Jobbatical, 'a great company, with good people'. It was the lifestyle itself. It started with a critique of the above-mentioned clichés. 'If you've ever tried to work from a beach then you know it's a pain in the ass,' he said. 'The sun is in your screen, and there's never good Wi-Fi. It's something people post on Instagram, but not what they do in reality. The life of a digital nomad isn't all cheap beer and rooftop parties. There are many more mundane aspects to it that nobody talks about because it doesn't fit the manicured image that social media has established. It's hard work. It's really hard to travel and to be truly productive. Every time you land somewhere, it takes a while to settle in and settle down. Even then, it takes crazy discipline. You're free to work when and where you like, but you still have to work just as much as anyone else, if not more. It takes over your life.'

Without a commute, an office to go to, or set work hours, Gonzalo described a world with no concrete barriers separating his personal and professional lives. They were blurred together into the same space, sometimes even the same room. For him, binge-watching YouTube or Netflix instead of doing work wasn't a joking matter but a real danger. In no time he could get sucked into an alternate reality that turned him from hard-working breadwinner to catatonic zombie. This all sounds rather familiar as I write at the end of 2020. Covid-19 has forced many office workers into a life much like the one Gonzalo describes. And with it, mental health problems, and Netflix subscriptions, have skyrocketed.

The opposite pitfall was the risk of never stopping. Switching off at the end of the day is a lot more challenging when the difference between work and home is shutting your laptop. 'There's always one more thing to do,' Gonzalo explained.

To combat this, he had developed an ascetic routine that he carried out no matter where he was in the world. He had two laptops – one for personal use, and another, stripped clean of any distractions, that he used for his job – and a wardrobe of professional clothes that he changed into every morning, despite rarely leaving the house, to get him into work mode. He even lugged around a coffee-maker just so he didn't need to change things up too much. The smallest changes could throw him off and lead to a whole day of work being wasted.

'When you work remotely, your employer's only way of measuring your performance is your productivity. So I have to be very strict with myself,' he explained.

This strictness eventually got the better of Gonzalo. He became despondent, dispirited, jaded. He initially ascribed it to breaking up with his Argentinian girlfriend, who was studying to become a fashion designer (she was his reason for being in Paris). But having gone back home to Argentina to find his bearings, he realised something much deeper and more serious was happening to him: 'I felt isolated, disconnected and disoriented in time and in space, never truly grounded or in communion with my surroundings. I had fled the rat race only to recreate it on the road. I was in a hurry and late at the same time, all the time. Never in "the now". I realised my Eldorado was making me miserable. I thought to myself: "What is the point of seeing the world if you don't actually *see* it?" I realised that my life had become one giant paradox. I was in a new country every few weeks, which in theory sounded great, but I had to force myself not to explore it to get my job done.'

In 2019, Gonzalo decided to settle down, and he did so in Barcelona, where he is building a newsletter media company with his childhood friend Franco from his hometown in Argentina.

•◆•

What few people realised then, and few still realise now, is how oxymoronic it is to suggest that nomadism is exclusively, even primarily, about mobility over great distances. Yet it is precisely the mobility aspect that appears to be one of the most fundamental aspects of digital nomadism. It's not simply doing your work at the beach; it's doing your work *at lots of different beaches* over a reasonably short space of time.

In 2013, at the age of twenty-four, Britain's James Asquith became the youngest person to travel to all 196 countries (after a short career in banking, he has since rather astutely launched the Holiday Swap app, which allows you to exchange homes over the holidays). The 23-year-old American Taylor Demonbreun spent most of 2017–18 trying to break Asquith's world record, as well as the 2015 speed record of Cassie De Pecol, a 27-year-old blogger from Connecticut who visited those same countries in just over eighteen months, blogging about her experiences on *TrekWithTaylor*. De Pecol funded her trip through endorsements and savings, costing her 'in total £160,000', and costing the planet an undetermined amount of greenhouse gas emissions. My favourite British conservationist, George Monbiot, will I'm sure be pleased to hear that De Pecol financed her trip by 'giving talks about sustainable tourism' and through promotions on her Instagram page.

Digital nomads are in a way the latest, broader and more inclusive iteration of a global elite, which is a big part of why young people, including my younger self, find the term and, on paper, the lifestyle so appealing. Building on Jacques Attali's caricatural take on nomadism-as-mobility in an age where mobility has been embraced by the privileged as the ultimate status symbol, in a 2004 article,[1] the late Harvard political scientist Samuel P. Huntington used the term

'Davos man' to describe a new breed of global elites. These gold-collared workers 'have little need for national loyalty, view national boundaries as obstacles that thankfully are vanishing, and see national governments as residues from the past whose only useful function is to facilitate the elite's global operations.'

.•.

Improving one's social and economic conditions remains an important lever of migration. Many new nomads from poor countries are still moving with an eye principally on lifting themselves and their loved ones out of poverty. And it is hardly surprising that, even in wealthier countries, young people seek to use technology and increased mobility to pursue some version of the American dream they are fed day in, day out, on social media, YouTube and Netflix, in their favourite series or the movies.

When considered against the backdrop of the housing bubble that formed after 2008 in many urban centres, including London, New York and Paris, location independence makes even more sense. If you are a twenty-something British graduate in the amazingly privileged position of being able to do your job from anywhere, and you want to save on your rent, it makes sense that you would pick Berlin over Bradford – Berlin has the cultural opportunities and services of a big, global city but, at least a few years ago, living costs there were closer to those in Bradford than an equivalently cool borough of London like Hackney. Economic vibrancy, trust and buying power all play a role in attracting the new nomads. But for a growing number of them, other considerations are coming into play, and even slowly taking over.

Many of the digital nomads I've spoken to experience some kind of existential crisis of the kind Gonzalo went through at some point. Not moving at all keeps our thinking narrow. It doesn't allow us to see the big picture, whether that's on a personal level, such as figuring out what we want to do with our lives, or the kind of large-scale thinking that we so desperately need to take decisive action against climate change. But what digital nomads have discovered in the past twenty years is that moving non-stop makes our thinking superficial and parasitic, and makes us disoriented: life becomes sad and overwhelming.

In part, this is because of a lack of community. When in constant motion, it is hard to maintain friendships and relationships. It's also hard to invest in a community when one does exist. I mean that in both the temporal and the financial senses. There are advantages to a place like Chiang Mai in having lots of young, comparatively rich Westerners around, but they are not necessarily paying taxes or investing in any direct way into the local economy, beyond buying coffees and beer. Equally, a couple of weeks is not long enough to make meaningful friendships with local people or to gain an understanding of their culture. Too often it is the case that digital nomads may be in Kathmandu, but are spending their time with other digital nomads. The backdrop may change, but the conversations they're having, and the people they're having them with, are not.

Furthermore, there is an environmental cost to this kind of frenetic, unthinking travel. The flight from London to Rome carries a carbon footprint of 234kg of CO_2 per passenger. That one reasonably short flight per person accounts for more CO_2 than is emitted by a citizen of Madagascar in a year. The cosmic scale of this unfairness is compounded when we consider that, today, Madagascar, one of the world's poorest countries, is already feeling the effects of climate breakdown, which is adversely impacting people's lives there right now to the extent that it's causing many of them to try to leave. Whereas we in the global North are currently blithely unaffected, and our migrations are an extension of our other luxuries. Though I have reduced my flying considerably, even before the pandemic, I haven't been able to square this circle thus far.

As I write this, the life of the digital nomad has been both disrupted enormously by coronavirus, and, also, reified for the rest of us. Covid-19 showed that working from home is possible for far more people than we expected. With hundreds of business closing their offices but maintaining their operations, it seems likely that many of these workers will not want to go back to the daily grind of either long commutes or small living quarters when the pandemic finally releases its grip. Similarly, many people have been laid off, meaning that the freelancers that swell the ranks of the digital nomads are in demand. On the other hand, with flights grounded, the mobility that defines the digital nomad's lifestyle has, albeit for only a moment, come to an end. With travel affected for the foreseeable future, it doesn't feel likely that the border-hopping of the past few years will continue unabated or unchanged.

There's another good reason why that might be. 'In times of crisis, people go back to family and friends and places where they have a high comfort level,' writes Steve King, a founding partner at Emergent Research, which has tracked the rise of the remote workforce since 2005. Citing increased health risks and the difficulty of crossing borders, King predicts that the free-ranging digital nomad lifestyle will be on hold until a vaccine is available. Anecdotal evidence suggests that 'the majority of digital nomads, in one way or another, have returned to their home country.'[2]

However, saying there is one 'good' way to be a migrant and suggesting that digital nomadism isn't it doesn't feel right to me. Much good can come of travelling around the world, seeing lots of different things, sampling all kinds of places and experiences. I think it makes more sense to look at the difference between Gonzalo's digital nomadism, and his life in Barcelona, as being two phases in life. The youthful, adventurous, hungry, exploratory phase gives way to a more appeased, simple, frugal one.

My sense is that nomadism is a capacious enough term and idea to contain both of these things. It can be about becoming a local, it can be about slowing down and about walking. Greater numbers of people will come to a more pronounced sense of localism and community following an experience of frenetic, high-mobility travel because such a migration creates a hunger for that rootedness. Essentially, the digital nomad was the prototype for what I think of as the New Nomad. They were the poster child for a global world and (with an unfortunate, but very understandable, youthful tendency to self-congratulation) showed the benefits of moving around. With time, however, their superficial approach to migration has proved unsatisfying. Rootless, they have forgotten that nomadism has always been a lifestyle rooted in the pasture: in locality, not just in motion.

While our environmental predicament certainly demands that we reconsider the pace of our global travels, asking young people to skip the adventurous phase and embrace the local directly is like asking a teenager to act like a parent. We need to offer the time and experience for people to grow, but we need to be able to do it in such a way that it doesn't degrade the environment. This is a huge problem; we're pulled in two totally opposing directions.

In the next chapters we'll look at ways to square the circle. Can we encourage nomadism and be environmentally responsible? Can we keep moving while respecting the places we are moving to or through? And what happens to those who stay?

9

A FIRE BRIGADE OF PYROMANIACS

'The descent to hell is easy.'

Virgil, *Aeneid*

There was an audible sigh of relief when the service ended. The congregation of First Southern Baptist Church started spilling out on the parking lot. People fanned themselves as the Midwestern sun beat down. Children in baggy shorts and faded T-shirts ran around while their parents mingled in groups of three and four. Annie watched as her two boys played with their friends. This was usually one of her favourite moments of the week. Everyone relaxed, chatting easily. The seriousness of the sermon giving way to the stuff of mundane, everyday life.

But on this early summer morning in 2018, Annie hung back. News had just broken that 2,700 children had been separated from their parents at the Mexican border as a result of Donald Trump's 'zero tolerance' immigration policy. She couldn't shake the image of children being held in cages like animals from her head. She had broken down on hearing reports of a Honduran man who had killed himself in his detention cell after his children were forcibly taken from him.

Annie, originally Anamari Garcia Ortega from Mexico City, and her husband Scott Boswell, a Kansas native, moved to Salina, a small city of 50,000 in the heart of the state, in 2008. Annie is a graduate of Tecnológico de Monterrey, Mexico's answer to the Massachusetts Institute of Technology in the US. As a graduate of this elite institution, a product of Mexico's upper-middle class, and the spouse of a neurosurgeon, she is not the sort of Mexican immigrant the average Trump voter thinks of when they declare support for building a wall. Still, as a brown-skinned Latina, she has been confronted with racism now and again since the couple settled in the Midwest fifteen years ago. She didn't expect moving to a small town in central Kansas to be any different from Kansas City or Nebraska, where she and Scott had lived before. But to her surprise, she had been welcomed into the community with open arms.

Salina is in a blue (Democrat) county in a sea of red (Republican) ones. Still, many of Annie's friends and fellow churchgoers are politically conservative and voted for Donald Trump in the 2016 elections. She had, occasionally, been hurt by some of the things that she had seen and heard during the heat of the campaign. People had posted comments on Facebook that had surprised and upset her. Annie and Scott are devout Christians, and she knew better than to let herself be overcome by anger or self-righteous indignation. She also knew that in a small community like Salina, a clash with a Trump supporter, or anyone for that matter, could have lasting consequences. So she kept her mouth shut and minded her own business.

But that morning was different. Something she had overheard earlier that day had got to her. In a discussion about what was going on at the border, people were rationalising the separation of children from their parents. Somebody had said, 'If people break the rules, they're going to suffer the consequences.'

'I took a deep breath,' Annie recalled. 'I knew this was one of those make-or-break moments; I was either going to lose them all or I was going to change their hearts.' She marched up to the group of adults and asked them to hear her out. She told them that she was hurt by what she had heard earlier. That even though she had accepted their way of life, assimilated to their culture and embraced it as her own, she was still a Mexican woman, too. That when she heard about the issues at the border as a Mexican, her heart bled for the way that her home country was being treated.

'You have learned to love me as a daughter and a sister. Some of you have taken care of my boys since they were three months old, treating them like your own. Now imagine that what's happening to those poor families at the border were happening to us – imagine that for some reason I got deported, or that I get separated from my kids without any idea where they'd gone. My children are half Mexican – don't you realise this could happen to them? This could happen to me!'

'There is no easy answer to what's happening at the border,' Annie continued. 'There's no magic one plus one equals two. But I want to ask one thing of you. You know me, and you've invested your time in getting to know me. You've seen the richness that I've been able to bring to this community because of where I'm from. So please, I beg you, don't forget that at the end of the day these are people. It's not abstract – these are real flesh and blood human beings that are being affected by these decisions. Real mothers, real fathers, real children. Don't take the humanity out of the problem; it's not an equation.'

The group stood speechless. Annie called her kids, grabbed Scott by the hand and said goodbye. In the days and weeks that followed, neighbours, friends and even members of the congregation she hardly knew reached out to the Boswells – and to Annie in particular – to show support and express affection. But Annie told me that by the expression on their faces that Sunday she already knew she'd gotten through to them. Even the enthusiastic Trump supporters were moved. She knew that she had been heard and that this community was her home.

•◆•

This chapter is about the pushback that immigration has received in recent years. Where is it coming from, and why? To answer, we're going to look in more detail at those who stay in the communities they come from. What are their concerns, and how might they be addressed? Unadulterated xenophobia exists, but much of the time hostility towards the foreign and the migrant is the result of fear of the unknown. Fear exploited for political purposes. As maps of the Brexit and Trump vote show, anti-immigration rhetoric plays best in places where there are few or no immigrants. There are those, too, who are afraid that their jobs might go to immigrants, who feel locked out of the global system, and are bothered by those people, often city-based, whom they feel get all of the benefits of migration that we've highlighted in this book. In the end, we'll ask, can we find common ground between those who move and those who stay?

In the twenty-first century, the big issues we face are collective ones that require collective solutions – chief among them climate breakdown. And, in the immediate term, climate breakdown is going to force more people to become migrants. We therefore desperately need to learn how to bridge the gap between those sceptical of the benefits of migration and those who can see them. Rather counterintuitively, the migrants themselves, like Annie, far from being the problem, are often part of the solution: they have a critical role to play in brokering a lasting truce between these parties. It won't happen magically, and it won't be easy. But people like Annie should give us hope.

Annie was credible and got through to people that day because of her reputation for kindness and generosity. Her compassion for fellow human beings isn't selective. She never gave up on immigrants, but she never gave up on Trump supporters, either. Annie's life is full of anecdotes of this kind, of attempts to bridge gaps between people. Franco Rivas, once a kid on a soccer scholarship that Annie helped by driving him to games, described to me how Annie would stop the car, drop everything and go buy clothes and food for the homeless people that they would come across as they drove around in the blistering Kansas winter, including many wearing confederate colours. Today, she does the same, whether they are wearing the ubiquitous *Make America Great Again* caps or not.

That summer day in 2018 was a transformative moment for Annie. It gave her a new faith in herself and in Kansas, a faith which wasn't dented by the fact that Donald Trump carried the state again in 2020. In the months that followed, she got involved in a campaign to help children of immigrants (so-called 'DREAMers', named after the Development, Relief, and Education for Alien Minors Act that was supposed to automatically grant them residency status but failed to pass in Congress) withstand the pressures of living under an administration that might kick them out of the country at any point. She got people in the community involved. She helped raise awareness of the pioneering role of Kansas Wesleyan University, the local college, in welcoming Latinx and African kids with a gift for soccer into the heart of America (she is one of the soccer moms far from home who follows, listens and supports these youngsters). She made local residents realise what an asset these kids were for the community, and cemented a new outlook on immigration for many.

Faced with Annie's cry for compassion, no one remained indifferent. What if, when it comes to immigration, the problem was more the messenger than the message? Annie's courage and humility, her tireless efforts to become a local, to integrate into her community, her sincere love of that community and the American Midwest in general, her readiness to honestly share her feelings and make herself vulnerable combined with her uncompromising defence of immigrants in need of support, all limited the attractiveness of the divisive discourse of nativists. It's easy to see that her potential as an agent of change in her community is far greater than that of your typical politician touring the state in the hope of garnering local support.

It wouldn't cross Annie's mind to vilify Trump supporters. For her, 'hate and racism are dis-eases [her hyphenation], symptoms of fear and anguish, not evil. You wouldn't wish harm on someone with a chronic disease, would you?' She sees people attracted to xenophobic discourse as people who are suffering. For her, 'liberals who sit at home watching talk shows that tell them they are on the good side of history and morality while scoffing at "the racist rednecks in fly-over states" are doing little good to the situation. If you want to change the world, invite a Trump supporter into your home for dinner ... We need to do both: To welcome the refugee and the Trump supporter into our homes. Scratch beneath the surface and you realise that far from being sick and tired of actual migrants, whom they hardly ever meet, people attracted to Trump here are brainwashed of course, but they are also, above all, sick and tired of being told that they are racist bigots by coastline elites who never set foot here but whose lifestyles they feel deep down – even though they aren't able to explain the ins and outs of how this is occurring – are threatening their own.'

Annie is pointing to one of the great paradoxes of our time: the most vocal proponents of immigration in our societies, who are in that position not because they are better people but because they are more urban, affluent and mobile, tend to think that it is about moral character. They don't see that open-mindedness and empathy for the migrant is a privilege, not a reason to be proud. These folks, if they are sanctimonious or contemptuous and unwilling to engage with those who are more reserved about migration, to go out of their way and actually sit down with them and talk about their problems and their fears, can end up fuelling much of the animosity towards abstract migrants. The problem is compounded when the same people who tell those worried that manufacturing jobs are going to other parts of the EU or the world that this is a good thing, follow up by suggesting any uneasiness they feel about immigration is simply down to them being racists.

As I listened incredulously to a Mexican immigrant describe her love for Kansas, the delicious irony of the situation wasn't lost on me. Here I was sitting in a café in Södermalm, Stockholm's manicured bourgeois-bohemian stronghold and a citadel of political correctness, pontificating about the virtues of travel as a means of overcoming prejudice, yet I myself was exhibiting extraordinary prejudice and condescension about a part of the world where I had never set foot. I simply couldn't wrap my head around the fact that a Mexican immigrant, who had been the occasional witness and victim of racism in the Midwest, as Annie told me she had, could be raving about what I dismissively thought of as 'Trumpland'.

It was so convenient to blame the people in that part of the country, the ones who had voted for Trump and seemed to hold dear everything that made me cringe about his America: ingrained misogyny, anti-immigration rhetoric, climate change denial, lack of gun control and staggering levels of inequality. But the truth is that I was just as ignorant as those I looked down on. I carry an American passport, and I identify as an American, but it took a loving, open-minded Mexican immigrant who refused to put labels on those who stay to make me realise how wrong I had been about the Midwest. Trump's election wasn't about racist chants, abortion and gun rights, or at least it wasn't just about that. It was about the bipartisan plutocracy that America had become, and about those who felt left out. And it was a reaction to modernity as a whole.

This contempt shown by liberals can be particularly pernicious and toxic because the nature of the liberal worldview is to deny that they are contemptuous of anyone. Contempt is not a progressive attitude, and therefore liberals, and I include myself in this, are not conscious that they are engaging in it, or will deny it when they are. Most Trump supporters wouldn't dispute that they 'Other' Mexicans, immigrants, Muslims or Democrats. That's why they vote for Trump. Their worldview not only accepts but takes pride in the fact that they are fundamentally different to those 'others'. But people like me, liberal-minded folk, have convinced ourselves that Othering is something that only racists and bigots do. Not us. The reality, of course, is that we spend just as much time as anybody else dividing the world into 'us' and 'them'. This asymmetry goes a long way to explain the extreme polarisation of our politics. Like Annie, I feel the onus is on liberals, who claim to reject Othering as a matter of principle, to go out of their way to bridge the divide.

Here we must pause and look at the great paradox of modern rhetoric on meritocracy. Barack Obama famously described himself as 'a skinny kid with a funny name who believes that America has a place for him, too'. Supporters have often claimed his election was proof of the fundamentally meritocratic nature of the US. Without skipping a beat, many of them went on to see in the election of Donald Trump proof of the fundamentally racist DNA of America. The truth is obviously more complex. The dubious claim that modernity is fundamentally meritocratic is being turned into a powerful weapon by nativist populists. In the past, those who stood at the bottom of the human pyramid were told that it was God's decision to put them there. Now, they are told that it is because they are failures, because they are dumb, lazy, or both.

What makes people vote for Brexit, Trump and similar populist measures or politicians is not privilege itself, but the fact that the privileged now believe they are more deserving of their success than elites of former times. This is the incredible irony of meritocracy. As the British Conservative thinker and author Toby Young has often said, when his father coined the term 'meritocracy', he did not see it as a good thing, for precisely this reason. Yet in the twenty-first century we have blurred its meaning and turned it into a form of self-congratulation. This is wrong. Meritocracy's claim to be a fair system makes those who don't succeed in it feel like failures, while it makes successful people feel like they are wholly deserving of and responsible for that success – that they've earned it. In other words, the unfairness of the system isn't the only problem. The problem is also that it purports to be fair. Elites of the past claimed superiority in an openly rigged system. Their 'merit' was that they had been 'chosen' by God. This was reason to be grateful, not reason to brag.

According to British sociologists Sam Friedman and Daniel Laurison,[1] this belief is held by many professionals of middle-class or wealthy backgrounds, even those with strong progressive politics: it's not necessarily that the poor get what they deserve, but that they themselves, personally, earned their high-status, prestigious jobs. Some version of the American dream – in France, for instance, it's called 'republican equality of chances' – has become consubstantial to modernity: the widely shared implicit belief, especially though by no means exclusively at the top of the social pyramid, that success and worth are nearly identical, that if you are really rich, you must be really smart and hardworking, and if you are poor, you must have messed up in some really big way.

What makes this such a political liability is the better-than-thou attitude that it leads to among elites, especially the tech-savvy, liberal or libertarian ones that thrive in the Silicon Valley or at Harvard. By dismissing the grievances and worldview of those who choose other ways of measuring their self-worth as lacking in ambition, by describing people focused on the local as simplistic, small-minded or archaic, the so-called learned antagonise them from the outset and lose all capacity to convince. They are reminiscent of the four horsemen of atheism (Christopher Hitchens, Richard Dawkins, Sam Harris and Daniel Dennett) who toured American campuses in the mid-2000s, purporting to be the heralds of religion's unravelling.

Overlooking faith's constitutive nature (being beyond Reason) and timeless writings on the subject from eminent figures as diverse as the philosopher Søren Kierkegaard, the physicist Niels Bohr and the psychoanalyst Carl Jung, the 'atheist bros' and their childish, boastful claims convinced no one who wasn't an atheist in the first place. To the contrary, they alienated many regular, decent people. Similarly, in our age of extreme political polarisation, this begs the question: what is the ultimate goal of politics? To convince those we disagree with or to feel good about ourselves for supposedly being 'smarter?' If it is the latter, liberals sure are doing a fantastic job.

•◆•

In June 2019, a cohort of American socialites, celebrities, media moguls and other captains of industry crossed the Atlantic in first-class cabins and aboard private jets to take part in Brilliant Minds, an annual conference organised in Stockholm by the wife of the former US ambassador to Sweden. The 2019 edition of the event was entitled 'Fluxability Quotient' [sic] and had as star speaker none other

212

than Barack Obama. According to the organisers, 'Fluxability Quotient' measured people's ability to 'move, shift, change, progress and flow strong with the current of the future', as well as 'sustainability in the art of constant transformation'. The core values celebrated were all laudable on paper: equality, transparency, social responsibility and 'a harmony of land and humankind'. Who wouldn't want a harmony of land and humankind?

Apart from Barack Obama, the guest speakers of the event included the CEOs of Snapchat and Buzzfeed, the former supermodel Naomi Campbell, the fashion designer Diane von Furstenberg, the actors Gwyneth Paltrow and Forest Whitaker, the rapper Cardi B, the chief content officer of Netflix, the heiress to the CBS Viacom media empire, the CEO of pharmaceutical giant Novartis … The list goes on and on.

As someone who spent years organising similar events, there is little doubt in my mind that elitist liberal gatherings à la Brilliant Minds, despite the ego-pleasing involved, are well-intended. The Brilliant Minds organisers really would sincerely like to move the proverbial needle in the right direction. Unfortunately, there is a hidden violence to that sincerity. Most of the time, not only do they fail to move anything in the right direction, but such events actually antagonise those who are the most sceptical of those values today. The fact that Barack Obama, arguably the single most iconic figure of contemporary progressive politics, could not see the fundamental problem of taking part in a closed event with and for very rich people in a five-star palace in

Stockholm speaks volumes to the blind spots privileged elites have regarding the discrimination that they too dole out.

The organisers of Brilliant Minds invited Greta Thunberg to give the opening keynote. She pointed out to those assembled that flying around the world in private jets to celebrate their own brilliance and pontificate about sustainability and 'making the world a better place' was denying reality. That contrary to what they seemed to think, this behaviour could actually be worse than saying or doing nothing at all.

But the time has come to acknowledge the violence of these good intentions. Violence is not only in the blows we strike; it is in our collective failure to meaningfully address the violence of our unfair present while purporting to be doing so. There is a terrifying violence in global elites' good intentions and their delusions about 'doing good', epitomised by their affection for the highly toxic oxymoron of 'green growth',[2] when the notion that a meaningful decoupling of growth and carbon emissions has ever happened is the subject of serious dispute, including by the *Financial Times*,[3] and while the single most accurate predictor of a country's, a company's, a household's or an individual's carbon footprint remains how much money they spend.

The time has come to pause and look at our tendency to compartmentalise issues and phenomena which are intricately related and to start connecting the dots between them. This in turn will allow us to understand that there is something deeply problematic in the worldview and the pro-migration stance of elites and how that pro-migration stance can become such a liability for those who migrate.

The migratory flows we have witnessed so far are but a taste of what's to come. Climate migrants are not an issue to worry about at some point in the future – they already exist, and in huge numbers. In 2018 alone there were 17.2 million displacements caused by natural disasters and around 764,000 caused by droughts.[4] Climate change is going to cause more natural disasters, and more droughts. For lots of people around the world, a push factor spurring them to migrate is already the climate. In the coming years, there are going to be more and more. The latest projections of the climate experts of the IPCC are that we may be looking at temperatures of up to six to seven degrees Celsius above pre-industrial averages by 2100.[5] This would make half the planet uninhabitable. It may sound far away. It isn't. A considerable number of humans already born will be around.

The problem isn't that liberal values, the value of human connection and open-mindedness, aren't part of the world-view of our Brilliant Minds. It's, again, that they end up thinking that open-mindedness and a pro-immigration stance are a testament to their good nature rather than their privilege and, more importantly, that these stances somehow in themselves move that proverbial needle. There was no discussion in Stockholm of the possibility that the attendees' affluence and ultra-mobility, and with it their open-mindedness, might on the one hand be predicated on the lack of affluence and mobility of others, and on the other that it may actually be causing disproportionate environmental damage and therefore indirectly contributing to climate migration.

There is something deeply immature about this *solution-ism* – the idea that all we need to do is put our heads together to 'come up with something' that will allow us to 'deal' with the main issues of our time. These issues, from migration to climate breakdown and the sixth species' extinction already underway, from the staggering levels of inequality of our world to the inherently ecocidal nature of the metastasising superorganism we call the global economy, are not 'problems'. They are predicaments. Problems have solutions, like the equations fourth-graders solve; predicaments don't. There are many ways to respond to predicaments, ranging from the healthy to the unhealthy, in gradations. But none of them is quick, easy or final. In this context, our modern tendency to look for 'solutions' isn't just misguided. It is a liability. We can't 'solve' these issues, however brilliant we may be. We need to live with them.

These predicaments also cannot be approached separately. Climate breakdown is fundamentally about energy and about the inequality of energy consumption. Inequality of energy use translates among others into mobility inequality. The most mobile people on the planet are the richest, and the richest people are the most energy-intensive and polluting. All of these things are connected. Purporting to address climate change without tackling inequality, in a world where 70 per cent of the world's greenhouse gas emissions are produced by the 20 per cent richest people, simply doesn't make any sense.

Meanwhile, most climate change deniers in the world today are not very mobile, and most of them hardly ever fly (though until recently of course, the most influential of them were in the Trump administration and the US Congress, and as such were extremely mobile). The staggering irony of our time is that the carbon footprint of most climate sceptics is insignificant compared to that of the average environmentally conscious privileged liberal, Brilliant Mind or not. The significant difference is that unlike the latter, the climate sceptics aren't prone to believing that they are part of the solution simply by virtue of their opinion. What if our biggest problem these days wasn't climate change denial as much as a denial of the laws of physics?

It's time for the ultra-mobile to realise just how much of a luxury and rarity flying actually is. The most serious guesstimates (from professional pilots) suggest that only 5–7 per cent of the world's population have ever flown.[6] According to the International Council on Clean Transportation, the 12 per cent of Americans who make more than six round trips by air annually are responsible for two thirds of global air travel.[7] In Britain, 70 per cent of all flights are taken by 15 per cent of the population.[8]

Meanwhile, those who fly and pollute the least are also the most vulnerable to the effects of climate breakdown. Africa's share of the global population is 17 per cent, but the continent generates only 4–5 per cent of greenhouse gas emissions. It is impossible to know what impact Covid-19 will have on these statistics in the long term. But, with the aviation industry facing a moment of existential threat, we have the opportunity to think strategically about what we want from the future of flying, and the future of migration.

With train travel, and slower travel, more practical during the pandemic, perhaps behaviour change will follow. More philosophically, with flights grounded, the coronavirus has reminded us just how exceptional flying is for the vast majority of humans.

When it comes to Brexit, Trump and the rise of far-right populism, the cognitive biases of liberals are just as hindering to our capacity to meaningfully address these issues as the cognitive biases of those who don't believe that the rise of the far right is a problem. If progressives are serious about promoting liberal values, human connection and the welcoming of foreigners, it is time we follow Annie or (harking back to the start of this book) Abdi's example and engage with those who are seduced by Trump and Farage – invite them over for dinner rather than pinch our noses and vilify or ignore them.

•◆•

In 2014, when she was eighteen years old, Berenice Tompkins walked from Los Angeles to Washington DC on an eight-month journey called the Great March for Climate Action. She met with one of those who'd joined her on her journey in 2015 in DC, who told her about another cross-continent walk that was planned in Europe later that year, led by Yeb Saño, a politician who had left the Filipino government to become a full-time climate activist. She decided to join Yeb and his People's Pilgrimage, which took participants from Rome to Paris ahead of the COP21.[9] She reiterated the experience in 2018, walking from Rome to Katowice in Poland for the COP24.

Walking across the US and Europe has allowed Berenice to meet some of the people who are most adversely affected by the intertwined economic, social and environmental imbalances that the global economy as we have organised it generates, and to do so on their turf. 'There are more of them [climate migrants] in Bangladesh, but there are many in the US, too. Walking is about building relationships, with them, with the other walkers and with the earth,' she tells me. It may sound lofty, but she sees this as pragmatism. 'The so-called realists who are running our countries are taking us straight to disaster. I have no time for that kind of realism.' As Berenice sees it, her nimble, grounded approach to nomadism is an important way to show 'the kind of elementary reverence for the ecosphere that just might save us; and in so doing, to become a genuine ecologist.'

She talks about her experiences on her blog *Climate Footsteps*: 'I feel I owe these stories to all of us who do not yet feel the impacts of climate change, who are hurting ourselves and others without really understanding what we are doing. When I mention to the person sitting next to me on the bus that I work on climate change, sometimes their eyes glaze over, or they look a bit confused, or they say, "Oh, you believe in that." Conservative think tanks and politicians have effectively convinced a large portion of the American public that climate change is like Santa, something you can choose whether or not to "believe" in. But it's much easier to deny an abstract scientific theory than to deny the experience, loss, pain of another human being.'

Young eco-nomads like Berenice have understood that the

way we treat the 'foreign' goes hand in hand with the way we treat nature. But she also understands something else that is fundamental. Climate activism, genuine nomadism, is not antithetical to migration. Climate activism is about moving around, it is about seeing more of the world, but doing so at a slower pace. 'In my experience, walking in nature is literally the ultimate self-reinforcing, transformative kind of climate activism,' Berenice tells me. 'Have you ever met someone who walks regularly – in nature, I mean, not up and down Broadway – who isn't passionate about nature and preserving it?' she asks me. 'Walking and doing things in nature should be an integral part of the basic curriculum for every American kid. Frankly, it's nuts that this isn't the case already.'

For Berenice, the marches she took part in allowed her to stop thinking of herself as fundamentally different from other people, just like Nicky, whom we met in Chapter 2, found himself identifying with the Continental Europeans he met on his travels as a Liverpool supporter: 'To me, "an African" is no longer an abstraction. It is my fellow earthling and friend Rabbi Ikola, with whom I crossed an entire continent on foot. But it's not only about breaking artificial boundaries with those you walk with. It is also about reaching out to the people that we don't or won't or can't reach out to when we stay caught up in our nine-to-five routines.'

Participating in the walks allowed Berenice to connect with like-minded people but also with people she would never have interacted with in New York. What she found changed her. She remembers 'one dude who spotted us on the road brought us firewood, adding: "I don't believe in this climate change thing, but if you're committed enough to walk across the country, I'll help you!" I feel I owe it to all these people to share their stories. Not just the ones who agree with me.'

In December 2018, having walked 1,500km, Berenice arrived in Katowice, where she met a young woman I once met sitting under an umbrella outside the Swedish parliament as I was passing by with my daughter and our Labs: Greta Thunberg. Together, they have laid the foundations of the climate youth movement. In terms of political weight, these new nomads might seem to represent very little. Stalin's question 'the Vatican, how many tanks?' comes to mind. But this hardly captures the momentum the transnational and translocal movements of climate protesters, many of whom are migrants or children of migrants, are garnering. In less than a year, they have grown from a few isolated cases, and in particular, a lone fifteen-year-old skipping school to sit outside the Swedish parliament protesting her government's inaction in the face of ongoing disaster, into what has arguably become one the most formidable vehicles of soft power of all times. All of it driven by the engine of a very special sort of migration.

·◆·

New nomads like Berenice are welcoming of technology and often humbled by it, but they don't treat it as an end in itself. They understand that the compartmentalisation of issues and phenomena which are actually intricately intertwined (whether due to a lack of awareness or outright denial of complexity) ruins our chances of constructively responding to them while making us unreasonably optimistic about our situation. They recognise that this unwarranted optimism, which has become the hallmark of modernity, has become toxic. They see that it can act like a drug which allows us to dance on the proverbial volcano and to sleep comfortably at night despite the reports we keep receiving about our house being aflame.

These reservations about technology and solutionism are aligned with a more rural worldview which isn't shared by urban liberals and global jet-setters. What if the healthiest responses to the rise of nativism and the politics of hate and the environmental and social crises we now face were far more likely to come from the more conservative (but also more conservationist) land rather than from more liberal, techno-enthusiast urban bastions?

Something profound happened to the human mind when the agricultural revolution turned us from an overwhelmingly nomadic species into an overwhelmingly sedentary one. The original meaning of 'economy' (οικονομός, oikonomós) was *management of the household*. The oxymoronic nature of the modern phrase 'global economy'– calling 'management of the home' the act of burning said home to the ground – has been lost on us for far too long. Facing our contemporary predicaments in a constructive way will not simply be about technological innovation. It will also be about bridging the gap between different conceptions of 'home', perceived as divergent when they are, in fact, complementary.

As people everywhere have noticed, confinement has been far easier for people in the countryside than it has been for people in the city, especially for those of modest means. This has led a number of people to rethink their priorities and to move out of cities. It is likely that many of them won't be going back. By allowing us to see that our contemporary obsession for ultra-mobility has corrupted our understanding of nomadism, the pandemic has enabled us to focus on all the other connotations of the term. In slowing us down, in forcing us to stay grounded and focused on our local environments and our respective communities, Covid-19 has created the conditions for a rapprochement between anywheres and somewheres, between nomads and sedentists. People like Annie and Berenice have a leading role to play in this.

Conclusion

Taking the Long Way Home

'I come into the peace of wild things who do not tax
their lives with forethought of grief . . . For a time I rest
in the grace of the world, and am free.'

Wendell Berry, 'The Peace of Wild Things'

I began this book with Abdi's story, and how his travels
opened up his world and the worlds of those he met on the
way. He personifies a sensibility that I have tried to artic-
ulate throughout. Namely, that the physical and outward
process of migration gives way to a much more important
internal journey, both for the migrant, and for the people the
migrant meets.

Migration is an amazing tool for facilitating the kinds
of connections we so urgently need to foster. Something
magical happens when you arrive somewhere you've never
been before. Everything that you need is in a bag you can
carry, and you are suddenly confronted by a multitude of

people – all of them totally different to you, but all of them, at least on some basic level, the same as you, too. Migration, the act of spending a meaningful amount of time away from where you were born, is the best tool that we have to learn to open our eyes and ears to other people. I hope this book has inspired you to go on an adventure with an open heart and see what you find along the road. Or if you are already a traveller, to embrace the marvel of slower, more conscious, geographical mobility. And I hope that in doing so you will discover, or perhaps rediscover, the importance of being a good host, to open your door, and your heart, to fellow travellers.

The coronavirus exposed the hidden precarity of the modern nomad – in a contingent world, where things can change at the drop of a hat, everybody needs a permanent place of safety and shelter. Being able to do your work from anywhere is only any good if you genuinely like and have a connection to the anywhere that you happen to be in. Covid-19, perhaps by necessitating social distancing, showed equally the importance of social contact. Many of us have now tasted the isolated life of the digital nomad, connected only via the internet, and its attractions are dubious. Location is just as important as ever, but chief among the draws of a place are the people with whom you share it. In short, rather than altering my opinions, the pandemic reaffirmed the things I had been thinking, and the journey that I had been on during the writing of this book. That is to say that, while travel broadens the mind and provides opportunities, this broadening and these opportunities are only maximised through sustained engagement with your new community, and a feeling of rootedness – both in where you are now and where you came from.

The experts at this maximisation are the new nomads. Why? Because they become experts at connection. When you turn up somewhere where you don't know anybody, you need to make connections quickly. Migration hones this skill, which is, I believe, innate in all of us, but can often lie more dormant in sedentary creatures. Emotional intelligence, the ability to connect, has felt even more important in recent months. Anecdotally, during this period of relative isolation, my more nomadic friends have found ways to maintain and even build new connections. Those whose lives have been more geographically circumscribed have struggled more with the disruption. Nomadism in the sense that I use it, giving equal weight to mobility and location, will be a key skill to develop as we face further disruptions this century – technologically, meteorologically and socially.

Many of the problems associated with migration today stem from a misunderstanding of the word 'nomad'. I first started hearing 'nomad' being used as a kind of buzzword in the past decade. It would be easy to point the finger at many of our contemporary problems with nomadism with technological and social changes that have occurred this century. But writing this book has forced me to zoom out and to see a misunderstanding of nomadism as part of a longer historical story.

For me, this process of zooming out has been, too, a product of migration. As I have travelled and moved around the world, my geographic horizon has broadened. But through my conversations with others, through learning about cultures different to my own, hearing new stories, and getting a richer, more granular understanding of the contemporary human condition, I have gained perspective on the human trajectory. This has allowed me to see the myopia, conceit and indeed even the racism of purporting to use the past few hundred years as the appropriate yardstick to measure human progress and decide where we might want to attempt to go from here. A shift in geographical perspective has led to a shift in my temporal perspective, too. For that reason, and particularly as we look to the future, I think it's worth thinking carefully about the origins of the word 'nomad', and looking again at the moment when humanity went from being a nomadic civilisation to a sedentary one.

Remember the notion that geographical perspective can feed into temporal perspective? The beginning of 'higher' life on earth is dated as beginning approximately 750 million years ago. Since that kind of timeframe is impossible to fathom (for us at least), let's cram it into just one year, as the plant-geneticist Wes Jackson taught me to, for the sake of the argument. On this scale, the first just-about animals, single-cell organisms, appeared around the time the pubs kicked out in the early hours of 1 January. Fast-forward to New Year's Eve 364 days later. It wasn't until 21:00, as the party started to pick up steam, that we became the anatomically modern human Sapiens. And not before 23:55 did we start mining carbon in the soil through agriculture and become sedentary creatures. As the ten-second countdown to herald a new year began, so too did the industrial age.

227

Viewed like this, our development since becoming a sedentary species, five minutes or 10,000 years ago, might be seen as an open parenthesis. Covid-19 allows us to pause, and consider whether we should close it. Before you ask, I am not suggesting that we go back to living in trees or caves. I am no neo-Luddite, and I am grateful for the many gifts bequeathed to us by the agricultural revolution. But the time has come for our civilisation to break with the Othering phase of our development, just as children do, and to start treating ourselves, each other and the rest of nature as different parts of the same metabolism.

We have spent the vast majority of our time on earth in small groups of less than one hundred nomads, on the move, certainly, but above all experts of the local. We were not under the modern illusion that our three-pound brains somehow made us radically distinct from our surroundings. We worked together. This wasn't a question of inclination but survival. If we failed to be attuned to our surroundings, we fell prey to predators or the elements. This, again, is what we risk doing: falling prey to the worst predators of all – ourselves – and the consequences of the intrinsic predatory and ecocidal nature of capitalism: the intricately intertwined evils of consumerism, greed, inequality and climate breakdown.

Looking to our post-Covid future, a reclamation of nomadism, one that is as focused on place and connection as it is on movement, gives me hope for both the future of migration and for the future of humanity in general. Nomadism comes naturally to us, more naturally than the sedentary lifestyles we've adopted more recently. We need to harness its power and become, like our forefathers, curious wanderers, connected to a community, living in harmony with our surroundings.

In creating a world imbued with affection and respect for the local and marvel for the entire ecosphere, with curiosity, humility, frugality, community and connection with each other and with nature at its heart, the new nomads, whose journeys have been charted in this book, have much to teach us. In the future, to build communities in an increasingly complex context, we are going to need the capacity to connect and network which allowed Lamine to find his way and eventually flourish in Spain. We're going to need the same openness and work ethic that allowed Abdi to thrive in Montana. We're going to need the same bravery that Charlotte had in moving to Colombia, the same pioneering spirit that caused Natsuno to flourish in Africa. The same enthusiasm that led Nicky to transcend hooliganism. The same curiosity that led Lulu to a life outside mainland China. The same connection and quiet wisdom Berenice earned on her walks. And the kind of charisma and people skills that caused Annie to change minds in the Midwest.

The new nomads have many things in common. What unites them and constitutes their – very real – education and privilege is the consequence rather than the cause of their mobility. They display a mix of awareness of their roots and a thirst for a granular understanding of the cultures they are immersed in. They remember where they come from *and* they know what leaving has done for them. Above all, they have all had the singular experience, somewhere along their journey, as their train left the station or the wheels of their plane left the tarmac and they looked out the window, as they walked along a dirt path or admired a sunset, of being overcome by a wave of boundless affection for humanity and all the earth's creatures and for this pale blue dot we call home itself. And all of them say that this emotion, sometimes fleeting, sometimes lasting, has changed them for ever.

My journey through the migrations of other people has taught me a general truth. All migrations, on some level, are a search for home. What a home is remains subjective and flexible and individual. Societies should have the same sort of suppleness as individuals to accommodate them, and to allow new communities to flourish. And, in the future, to create a world in which migrants are welcomed, where migration is made possible and easy for those who need it most, and where those who choose not to migrate are made to feel part of a globalising world, rather than apart from it, we need to do everything we can to foster these new ways of living.

So, for me, it's not simply about accepting that there will be more migration. I actively embrace it. But I actively embrace a better, greener, and therefore slower, migration. I call for a rejection of the binary local vs global dichotomy. We can be grounded in a local culture and aim for universal ideals. We have to. Contrary to what populist politicians would have us believe, the global realm isn't just about Davos, elitist jet-setting or international trade. The global realm is also about an ethic which holds that white working-class aspiring nomads in Hull, the American Midwest or Bulgaria, the mature Bangladeshi tradeswoman and the immature Canadian YouTuber, the Guarani of the Amazon and the teenage daughter of Vietnamese boat people, the Yemeni and the Venezuelan refugee, all have an equal claim to freedom and safety in and from the world, and a recognition that each has much to offer to the other.

It's not vanity to think the inner is connected to the outer, it's clarity.[1] To reconnect with nature, we must reconnect with each other. To reconnect with each other, we must reconnect with ourselves. To reconnect with ourselves, we must, in some way, become the new nomads, and start out on the long way home.

POSTSCRIPT

'The limit of political possibility today is the number
of people who can sit around a table and share a meal
together.'

Ivan Illich

Having spent over three years researching and writing this
book, it occurred to me that all this talk about what a new
kind of nomadism might look like needed to be translated
into action. In recovery from addiction, I have often been
told, 'you can't think yourself into healthy action; you have
to act yourself into healthy thinking.' So it is for nomadism.
This is how Black Elephant came into being.

The first time Abdi and I met in person was not on a
Montana ranch but at the World Economic Forum in Davos
in January 2017. I was heading the global expansion of a
cybersecurity firm (and about to be fired for being a tad too
candid on Twitter about what I thought of the newly inaugu-
rated president) and had heard of a Malian student who had

risen from a rural background in Africa to studying at one of the world's top universities. He sounded like the perfect spokesperson for a campaign for a global youth work visa that I had convinced my sceptical CEO of launching. We called it the New Nomad Visa.

I have taken many people to Davos over the years, from political dissidents and Nobel laureates to rappers, from famous writers and journalists to CEOs. It's quite an intimidating environment. I assumed Abdi would be like a fish out of water. Instead, the slim, athletic, bespectacled Malian struck me by his capacity to stay clear-headed in the moment, to take it all in and enjoy himself. When prompted to tell his story and explain why he was there (the main activity of everyone at the WEF), he took his time to think before speaking. In an environment where everything is rushed, he was not afraid to move slowly. You know the saying 'don't just stand there, do something'. Abdi seemed to know the value, sometimes, of just standing there. Seeing him in action was the beginning of my understanding of what I mean by the title of this book.

People in Davos loved Abdi. And they loved the story of Abdi going from the farmhouse of his youth in Mali to Stanford and onwards to Davos. His presence in Davos was proof that they were open-minded. That there was real diversity in Davos.

But while he welcomed the experience and remained engaged and friendly at all times, Abdi knew better. When we debriefed the trip in San Francisco a few months later, he told me about his experience at Ranch Sieben. I immediately

233

understood what he was getting at. What was missing in Davos was not Wunderkinds like himself, regardless of their religion and skin colour. It was people like Aaron and Jeff. Davos' postcard diversity was a caricature. The local was remarkably absent.

What Abdi had understood was that the reason he was popular in Davos was that despite being a Black Muslim, he represented something familiar for global elites, something they were accustomed to celebrating: the hero's journey, the meritocratic myth, the American dream. To those he encountered, it seemed to go without saying that the most exciting thing about his life was that he had started in rural Africa and ended up talking to them. What he instinctively felt was that his capacity to connect with Trump-supporting Aaron and Jeff was just as important. And that his childhood walks to the family farm played an instrumental and indeed far more essential part in this than his Stanford education.

As I conclude this book, having ranged around the world and heard the points of view of both those who speak out against migration, and those who are themselves migrants, I feel more convinced than ever that we have the most to learn from those who are least like us. We must engage with the other until we are able to appreciate our common humanity. The new nomads have a vital part to play in this process of engagement between anywheres and somewheres.

In the global forums we have used so far to organise the global conversation, from Davos to the UN, our instinct has been to seek and focus on the lowest common denominator, the subjects and the positions that would raise no eyebrows.

This is understandable when you are seeking to avoid conflict between parties with potentially widely divergent views. But it comes at a cost: you might end up with a parody of diversity around the table; a lack of willingness to talk about the real issues at hand; as a consequence, the consensus you reach may be weak and meaningless, and can end up alienating human societies at large. This is precisely what has happened to Davos and the UN.

In March of 2020, as we sat in confinement in the first months of the coronavirus pandemic, Abdi and I got together on Zoom. We brought in many other new nomads, too, and started talking about that phrase we've all heard so many times since the beginning of the pandemic it has almost lost its meaning: 'This changes everything.'

We had both read articles and essays by the great minds of our time along those lines, and in the months that followed, we realised that this literature didn't age well. But we also felt, deep in our gut, that there was a there there. That this crisis, the pandemic, was also an opportunity to address the myriad other crises we face. That in this unique moment in the human trajectory, as we were for a moment at least in the same headspace, we needed to try something new.

What if, we thought, we brought people together whose worldviews are *truly* at odds, and instead of seeking the lowest common denominator, we went for the highest? What if the most realistic way to bring about the consequential change our current, unsustainable, indeed apparently suicidal, course demands, was to go for the elephant in the room?

That's how, together with other new nomads whose adventures you have followed in this book, like Natsuno who is now studying at Oxford and Lamine who is still driving his cab in Barcelona, we founded Black Elephant.

Black Elephant is a rare, magical pachyderm born in confinement, somewhere between a platformless media, an artistic current, a think tank and an influence ecosystem. The name is derived from Nassim Taleb's *Black Swan*, an unforeseen event with momentous consequences, as some people have taken to describing Covid-19. But for decades now, countless experts have been warning us that such a pandemic was bound to happen. The coronavirus is hence not a black swan but rather what happens when the elephant in the room crashes the party and defecates on the dinner table. It is what happens when we choose to ignore the unsustainability of our civilisation's present course.

At root, the point of Black Elephant is to facilitate conversations, and our basic building blocks are what we call Black Elephant parades (the technical term for a herd of elephants) bringing together ten to fifteen people on average. These parades started out and continue to happen on Zoom but have also been taking place in person in people's kitchens and living rooms and in restaurants around the world.

Black Elephant parades are fundamentally about breaking with antiquated hierarchies and siloed thinking. No big names pontificating while others listen quietly. They serve as an agora where somewheres and anywheres of all kinds can meet: a place where intellectuals, farmers, artists, schoolteachers, refugees, Trump supporters, corporates, techies, patriots, ecologists and collapse theorists can meet and listen to each other. A place where eclecticism in all its forms, honesty, candour and respect for Otherness are the rule.

Apart from the search for low-hanging consensus, the other unspoken rule of convening gatherings with people of diverging views has been that the organisers needed to be objective. We believe this claim to objectivity isn't credible, nor desirable. Dennis Meadows and his team published *The Limits of Growth*, a book which used computer modelling to argue that we had a growth problem. Fifty years later, the main conclusion of the WEF's 2020 gathering was that . . . we have a growth problem.

As we set out to build our pachyderm, we felt it was time to admit that there is little that is objective about the globalist worldview. Instead, what we new nomads needed to do was to combine radical forward-thinking with open-mindedness, humility and a willingness to move slowly, both intellectually and physically; an acute awareness of our fundamental ignorance regarding most things (and of the fact that what we know will likely always be infinitely inferior to what we don't know) and that what we hold to be true today is unlikely to hold true tomorrow; the celebration of honesty and open-mindedness; and the willingness to listen to and engage with those we disagree with, especially those whose views make us particularly uncomfortable.

The editorial line of Black Elephant is thus founded on a single professed ambition: to question the narratives that modernity would have us take for granted. Above all, it calls on us to question our tendency to describe the myriad crises of our time (from Trump and Brexit all the way to financial crises, hurricanes and of course Covid-19) as deriving from external, exceptional threats to an otherwise fundamentally functional system and to consider instead, as the Brazilian scholar Vanessa Andreotti encouraged us to on our very first parade, the possibility that these crises might more accurately be described as the product of the violent, unsustainable practices required to build and sustain modern civilisation.

As the brainchild of nomads who are in the business of engaging with sedentists, Black Elephant is also focused on decrypting complexity, shedding light on the relationship between people, places and phenomena which we have found convenient or reassuring to think of as distinct but which can only be understood as part of the same metabolism. In the new era opened by Covid-19, the whole world has understood that what happens in Wuhan is, once and for all, everybody's problem. But so is what happens in the mines of eastern Congo, where many of the rare earth metals contained in our smartphones and tablets are extracted, in the refugee camps of the island of Lesbos and in the Amazon forest.

In one of the first Black Elephant parades, Cooper Hibbard, the owner and manager of the Montana ranch where Abdi landed in 2016, explained how he had been too busy dealing with a parasite which had been ravaging his herds to think about the pandemic – until he realised that humanity and his herds were in some ways just as vulnerable to the whims of nature.

On the call was Sigurlína, an Icelandic woman who was once the senior producer of Star Wars Battlefront and FIFA World Cup, two of the world's most successful video games franchises, who was joining us from Orange County, just south of Los Angeles (she has now moved back to Iceland). These two chatted animatedly with one of the sweetest, most serene human beings I know. Based in Portsmouth, Tola is a reformed gangster and former prison convict of Caribbean and Nigerian descent who now helps addicts find their bearings in recovery from drug and alcohol addiction by offering them a job working for his catering business. Also on the call was a young firebrand nationalist from the Netherlands, the former Brazilian Minister for Foreign Affairs, the French founder of Doctors without Borders and a young Congolese woman named Emmanuella, the founder of the Kinshasa-based NGO Ma Voisine (My Neighbour), who was raped when she was four and again during her adolescence, and who figured out that the only way she could begin to heal from the trauma of the sexual and physical violence she endured was to help other girls who have gone through similar experiences. We brought very different backgrounds and trajectories to the table. We had different political views and different ideas about the future. But all of us were committed to listening *to* and engaging constructively *with* each other.

•◆•

Like so many other institutions, the World Economic Forum was knocked out of whack by the pandemic. In August 2020, the decision was made to cancel the upcoming annual meeting in January. At the time of writing, it has been replaced by an exceptional meeting in Singapore in May 2021. As a recovering Davos addict, I think the time has come to shut it down.

For five decades now, the WEF has been paid hundreds of millions of dollars by the world's most profitable companies to not have a serious, painful conversation about our addiction to growth. Just as for an alcoholic uncle, an intervention is called for. It's illusory to believe it can be summoned by the people with the best dope in the game.

The end of Davos has been predicted many times before, but there is reason to believe this historical moment could prove fatal to the WEF. As an advisor to tens of political leaders and CEOs of multinationals over the years, I know one of their best-kept secrets: that 90 per cent of their bandwidth is devoted to sounding smart – or, at the very least, not looking stupid. Since the beginning of this pandemic, every single one of them has been thinking hard about one thing above all: how they are going to tell the story of the world and their story and that of their company, their brand, their product or their party in the coming months and years in such a way that they can prove that they received the proverbial memo; that they 'get' the fact that Covid-19 has opened a new era.

They are trying to figure out how they are going to prove to the world that their corporation or their government has understood that 'going back to normal', whatever that is supposed to mean, is not an option and that the world of tomorrow will not, indeed cannot, be the same as the world of yesterday. I can't say for sure how they can prove they get it. But what *is* sure is that there is a very simple way for them to show that they *don't* get it. And that is by going back to Davos.

In the twentieth century, geopolitical summits like Versailles and Yalta laid the foundations of the world order. Bretton Woods and Davos were geo-economic, too. The new era opened by Covid-19 will require a new kind of decentralised gathering, perhaps best described as geosocial and nomadic. Instead of being exclusive and excluding, it might include not just politicians, CEOs and NGOs but also randomly selected representatives of local and translocal, professional, indigenous, etc., communities.

Instead of seeking meaningless consensus at the top of the mountain, it might meet down in the plains and search for the highest common denominator: the elephant, or rather the parade of elephants, in the room, starting with our addiction to growth and carbon and the structural inequality they mechanically foster. Instead of cramming delegates inside a congress centre, it will consist of small, eclectic groups taking walks in the countryside so as to oxygenate brains, do away with hierarchies and create a new sense of intimacy and humility among the walkers. After wandering together for a mile or two, a CEO, a political leader, a schoolteacher and an activist are just four pilgrims.

The time has come for a new vision for humanity and a new kind of gathering to embody it. Abdi, my other pachyderm friends and I believe that Black Elephant and the new nomads can play a role in helping such a new kind of gathering to emerge.

ACKNOWLEDGEMENTS

'Ever tried. Ever failed. No matter. Try again.'

Samuel Beckett

Addicts are immature, impatient creatures. I am no exception. Writing this book has been by far the toughest and the most rewarding process I have ever gone through. It has taught me about myself and this pale blue dot of ours. I used to think life was about the sprint. I used to think writing was about the sprint. I thought this book would be done in months and, as the months turned into years, I went through moments of despair that reminded me of my worst moments in active addiction. The French author Georges Bernanos held that the highest form of hope is despair overcome, and indeed here I am, four years later, full of gratitude and hope and with the beginnings of a legacy to pass on to my children.

None of this would have been possible without Faith. I was a die-hard agnostic most of my adult life and there is not the slightest doubt in my mind that I would long be dead

243

if it weren't for my Higher Power, which, despite Spinozan leanings, I call Allah. My relationship to God is the most important thing in my life.

This book wouldn't exist without Aurore Belfrage. You put up with all my insanity, immaturity, grandiosity and, well, my bullshit. You picked me up, time and time again. You encouraged me when I was alone, lost in the snow like Hans Castorp. Husbandry doesn't come naturally to me. Day after day, you showed me the way, diligently mothering and providing the loving care our daughter deserves. More than most, you walk your talk.

I would like to express my eternal gratitude and love to Samia Benammou, who took care of me and my siblings and here and there still babysits our own children, nurturing us all with her unconditional love and support. Thank you, Samia, for the self-confidence you instilled in me and for allowing me to see the beauty of Mediterranean cultures and Abrahamic traditions.

I wouldn't have made it thus far if it weren't for my extraordinary parents and siblings, Max, Charlotte and Jojo, who put up with the exhausting, hopeless, often unbearable adolescent and attention-seeking missile I remained for most of my adult life, and can still turn into when I don't work my programme. I love you more than words can say.

Children of alcoholics and addicts don't have much choice but to mature early. I haven't robbed you of your entire youth Oscar, Alhamdulillah. Know that I am incredibly proud of the man you are becoming. Remember to stay aware of where you are in space and time. And take good care of your siblings.

A very special shout-out to my extended family: my nieces Calliope, Mina, Magdalène and Mathilda; my goddaughter Beatrix and her sisters Margot and Violet; Oscar's sister Victoire; Auntie Chris, who held my hand and warmed me with her quilts and her love throughout life; her solid rascal of a husband, Ed, and my cousin Anton, an absolute gem of a human being; the sensational Uncle Kirk and Aunt Peggy, always there for me in San Francisco; Tante Nicole and fam in Hamburg; Cornelia, Willi, Miriam and Christian as well as Rudiger and Sabine in Frankfurt; Didi, Tony, Hugh and Brian in Dublin; Paolo, *fratello mio*; Virginie, Mehdi and Domi; Nadeah, Steve and Kristina; Granny, Florence, Papouli, Opa; Franzi, Tante Charlotte, Oncle Pétère, Mimi and of course, all the Belfrages. I love you fam.

I would not have made it thus far without my best friend, Henry Mainwaring, and his far better half Jennifer, who at decisive moments of my life, loved me when I couldn't love myself. You kept me going when I was at my lowest by trusting me with what you hold dearest. Over the years, you taught me the value of service to others, earnestness, humility and propriety.

Writing a book is actually re-writing and pruning, as I found out the hard way. I am deeply grateful for the stellar insights, editorial advice and ongoing support I have benefited from in the process of bringing this one to life. I'm forever indebted to my agent Gordon Wise at Curtis Brown and to Ian Marshall at Simon & Schuster in London. I would like to give a special thanks to Sasha Polakow-Suransky for helping me find my voice, to Jack Ramm for helping me get the manuscript across the finish line and to Adam Strange for his enthusiasm and sharp copyediting. Maria Paz Acchiardo played an essential role, too, thanks to her wisdom as an experienced nomad and healer.

Thanks to Eleanor Fielding for her help with the research and to Christy and Robert Tanner, Robbie Harb, George Masselam, James Barlow, Betsy Devine, Louise Schwingel, Max Alletzhauser, Alan Riding, Paul Berman, François Esperet, Jeremy Thomas, Sophie des Déserts, and Aurélien Bellanger for reading chapters of this book early on and providing constructive criticism. And a big thank you also to David Winner and Marianne Brooker for helping me understand I needed to stop trying to get others to do my work.

I would also like to extend my sincere thanks to the nomads I met and interviewed in the process of researching this book, many of them at length, for their precious time and invaluable insights: Habib Kazdaghli; Alhaji Siraj Bah; Farzad Ban; Alia Wingstedt; Max Karlsson; Niall Saville; Emmanuella Zandi; Ankit Desai; Tania Beard; Paola Audrey; Ciku Kimeria; Jan H. Christiansen; Miguel Jonsson; Catherine Mayer; Alok Alström; Arnaud Castaignet; Gwamaka Kifukwe; Karoli Hindriks; Aida Hadžialic; Ibrahima Tounkara; Ben Sock; Yeb Saño; Greta Thunberg; Vic Barrett; Sani Tahir; Vybarr Cregan-Reid; presidents Kersti Kaljulaid and José Ramos-Horta; Joi Ito; Guyonne de Montjou; Max Ajl; Lu Gigliotti; Ramazan Nanayev; Julien Rochedy; Sigurlína Ingvarsdóttir, Peter Smith, Nic Cary and Xen Herd; Kevin Anderson and Keri Facer; Nasita Fofana; Ayşem Mert; Gareth Dale; Phoebe Tickell; Lennart Olsson; Stan Cox, Bryan Thompson, Pheonah

Nabukalu and Fred Iutzi at the Land Institute; Sohnia van der Puye; Ilse van der Velden; Ben Anderson; Spencer Wells; Glenn Chisholm; Beta Grétarsdóttir; Eva Vlaardingerbroek; Efua Oyofo; Muyabwa Moza; Harper Reed; Anna-Hope Kabongo; Karim Sy and Keita Stephenson; Niki Jaiswal; Sophia Rashad; Matt Yanchyshyn; Matteo De Vos; Patrick Chadwick; Monika Karapetian; Nour Sharara; Gordon Cyrus; Paul da Silva; Asad Hussein; Assa Traoré; Noura Berrouba; Rabbi Stephen Berkowitz; and last but not least Franco Rivas.

This book is also the fruit of love and affection: that of Aco Mitteräcker and Annette, my family in Vienna; Christophe de Margerie and Adrien Pochna, *reposez en paix mes frères*; Jérémie Sfez and Samuel Todd, my doppelgängers; Erwan Templé; Hadj Khelil; Julien and Caroline Galinié; Anne and Jeanne Fagnani; Toma Damisch; Behrang Behdjou; David Saffar; Mehdi Mahmoudi; Pierre-Yves Thieffine; Arnaud Roth and Juliette Bonté; Arnaud Garnier and Caroline Normand; Giacomo Clerici; Martine and Micke Ribbenvik; Walter Huyhn, Mark Payne, Tola Gisanrin and my sponsors Dom and Brendan; Saga's godmothers, Betsy Devine and Emma Winberg; Djamel Boumaza; Jamel Benrabaa; Seb Bellwinkell; Trix and Robert Heberlein; Therese Larsson; Natalie Jeremikenko; Harald Pühringer, Andreas Papp, Thomas Sautner and Heinz Reiter; Kevin Slavin and Lisa Mosconi; Annika Hedås Falk; Anne-Laure Kiechel; Antti Niemi and Irina Shryna; Richard Bean; Lorena Chamorro; Baratunde Thurston; Andrew Adonis; Hilary Mason; Cheryl Contee; Péguy Luyindula; Alia Ibrahim; Amanda Parkes; Giulio Uggiano; Paps, Brasco, XLO and Mokless;

Harald Vlugt; Zouhair Ech Chetouani; Elhadgi Gueye and Khoudia Dionna; Celso Amorim; Eric Pape; Damien Loras; David Brunat; Mamuka Kudava; Nico Mougenot; Safia and Dominique Camilleri; Emna and Bassem Bouguerra; Arabella Dorman and Dominic Eliot; Dayo Olopade and Walter Lamberson; Sandra Arigoni; and Usman Haque.

A special mention for Anne Berest, Aki Kuroda, Olivier Guez, Oxmo Puccino, Marc Lambron, François Samuelson, Emmanuel Carrère, Simon Kuper, Denise Marie and Éric Naulleau for taking me out for lunch or dinner when no one else in Paris would.

The quiet and slow-moving pachyderm we call Black Elephant was supported from day zero by my co-instigators Jean-Manuel Rozan, Bill Vitek and Loïs Henry, as well as by Anton Mifsud-Bonnici, Muriel Dube, Dijana Duvnjak, Fatoumata Sy, Eugenio Molini, Robert Hutchinson, Natalie Paret, Alexandra Palt, Rebecca Enonchong, Xavier Niel, Ian Rogers and Marion Darrieutort.

My culture isn't national but rather made up of a smorgasbord of localities. Fittingly, *The New Nomads* was written in several of them. My eternal gratitude goes to Helena and Frank Belfrage for their unfailing kindness, hospitality and elegance and for opening their homes to me in Dalarö and Bonnieux. Thank you to Athena Sidiropoulou, to the Grikos gang and to all my fellow Patmians. A special thanks to Sébastien Pennes for opening his home to me in Ustaritz, to my mom for doing so in Lourmarin, to my sister Charlotte in Montreuil and to Grégoire Chertok in Paris, when I was broke. *Ça ne s'oublie pas.*

I am deeply indebted to Jean-François Rischard for his trust over the years and to Jean-François Revel, whose chutzpah and impertinence were instrumental in helping me climb the magic mountain. I am even more indebted to the quiet radicals Wes Jackson and Wendell Berry, whose warmth, wisdom and poetry guided me gently back down to the plain. I am also grateful to Satish Kumar, Adnan Ibrahim, Bill Vitek, Ghaleb Bencheikh, Corine Pelluchon, Vanessa Andreotti, Dougald Hine and Tareq Oubrou for their generative input. You have all taught me to fail better.

I would like to express my eternal gratitude to all the friends and friends of friends of Bill and Bob with whom I have the privilege of treading a path beyond my wildest dreams, one day at a time.

Finally, I would like to give a shout-out to Ewelina, Sam, Rein, Milky, Alex and Ed at Prufrock Coffee; Nicolas at Telescope; Johanna and the entire team at Drop Coffee: Giacomo, Leia, Catarina, Amanda, Robin, Matt, Jean, both Lisas, Felipe, Veronica, Sievert and, of course, Mo; Sergei, David, Katya, Markus, Vincent and Jonathan at Johan & Nyström; Gödze and Nikos at Pernera; Nicolas at Le Tinel in Bonnieux; Tina and her team at Dalarö Bageri; Hami and Robin at Organico in Söder; Ben at Mana Coffee in Aix; Christos and Kostas at Samba Coffee and Christos at Anana in Athens; and last but not least, Nobuaki and Oliver at Democratic Coffee in Copenhagen. Thanks also to Ed Anderson Brown and Nena Dimitriou.

Last but not least, I would like to express my love and gratitude to Ta, *agapi mou*, Izzy-Banana and Stormie.

249

BIBLIOGRAPHY

The Holy Bible. Hendrickson (2003).

The I Ching or Book of Changes. Translated by Richard Wilhelm. Princeton University Press (1967).

The Quran. Translated by M. J. Gohari. Quran Institute (2007).

The Talmud. Translated by Joseph Barclay. John Murray (1878).

AA World Services, *Alcoholics Anonymous.* New York (2002).

Akomolafe, B. *These Wilds Beyond Our Fences: Letters to My Daughter on Humanity's Search for Home.* North Atlantic Books (2017).

Anderson, B. *Imagined Communities: Reflections on the Origin and Spread of Nationalism.* Verso (1983).

Andreotti, V. *Hospicing Modernity.* North Atlantic Books (2021).

Andreotti, V. *Actionable Postcolonial Theory in Education.* Palgrave Macmillan (2011).

Andreotti, V., Mario, L., and T. M. de Souza.

Learning to Read the World: Through Other Eyes. Global Education (2008).

Arendt, H. *The Origins of Totalitarianism.* Mariner Books (1973).

Saint Augustine. *The City of God.* Hendrickson (2009).

Aymé, M. *Les Contes du Chat Perché.* Gallimard (1969).

Aymé, M. *Uranus.* Gallimard (1948).

Baker, C. *Navigating the Coming Chaos: A Handbook for Inner Transition.* iUniverse (2011).

Balibar, É. *Race, Nation, Class: Ambiguous Identities.* Verso (1991).

Barthes, R. *Mythologies.* Translated by Annette Lavers. Cape (1972).

Bastani, A. *Fully Automated Luxury Communism: A Manifesto.* Verso (2019).

Benjamin, W. *Theses on the Philosophy of History* in *Illuminations.* Translated by Harry Zohn. Schocken Books (1968).

Berlin, I. *The Power of Ideas.* Vintage Digital (2012).

Berry, W. *A Place In Time: Twenty Stories of Port William.* Counterpoint (2002).

Berry, W. *A Place on Earth.* Counterpoint (2001).

Berry, W. *Home Economics: Fourteen Essays.* North Point Press (1987).

Berry, W. *Life is a Miracle: An Essay Against Modern Superstition.* Counterpoint (2000).

Berry, W. *The Art of the Common Place.* Counterpoint (2002).

Berry, W. *The Unsettling of America: Culture & Agriculture.* Sierra Club Books (1986).

Berry, W. *The Way of Ignorance.* Emeryville, California: Shoemaker & Hoard (2005).

Berry, W. *The World-Ending Fire.* Allen Lane (2017).

Berry, W. *What Are People For?* Rider (1991).

Blyton, E. *Five Go to Mystery Moor.* Hodder Children's Books (1997).

Bohr, N. *The Philosophical Writings of Niels Bohr.* Ox Bow Press (1987).

Bourdieu, P. *Distinction: A Social Critique of the Judgement of Taste.* Translated by Richard Nice. Harvard University Press (1987).

Bouvier, N. *The Way of the World.* Translated by Robyn Marsack. Eland (2011).

Braudel, F. *A History of Civilizations.* Translated by Richard Mayne. Penguin (1995).

Braudel, F. *The Mediterranean in the Ancient World.* Translated by Sian Reynolds. Penguin (2002).

Bulgakov, M. *The Master and Margarita.* Translated by Michael Glenny. Collins and Harvill (1974).

Caro, R. A. *Working: Researching, Interviewing, Writing.* Albert A. Knopf (2019).

Carrère, E. *Limonov.* Translated by John Lambert. Penguin (2014).

Céline, L-F. *Journey to the End of the Night.* Translated by Ralph Manheim and Angela Cismas. New Directions (2006).

Chatterton Williams, T. *Losing My Cool: How a Father's Love and 15,000 Books Beat Hip-Hop Culture.* Penguin Press (2010).

Chatterton Williams, T. 'The Next Great Migration'. *The New York Times* (27 February 2015).

Choamsky, N. *Who Rules the World?* Penguin (2016).

Clemens, M., and Postel, H. *Deterring Emigration with Foreign Aid: An Overview of Evidence from Low-Income Countries. Population and Development Review 44.* Wiley-Blackwell (2018).

Cox, S. *Any Way You Slice It: The Past, Present, and Future of Rationing.* The New Press (2013).

Cox, S. *The Green New Deal and Beyond: Ending the Climate Emergency While We Still Can.* City Lights (2020).

Cregan-Reid, V. *Primate Change: How the World We Made is Remaking Us.* Cassell (2018).

Davis, M. *Late Victorian Holocausts: El Niño Famines and the Making of the Third World.* Verso (2001).

Debord, G. *The Society of the Spectacle.* Black and Red (1970).

Dostoevsky, F. *The Idiot.* Translated by Alan Myers. Oxford University Press (1992).

Durkheim, É. *Suicide: A Study in Sociology.* Translated by John A. Spaulding and George Simpson. Routledge & Kegan Paul (1952).

Durkheim, É. *The Division of Labour in Society.* Translated by W. D. Halls. Free Press (1997).

Eisenstein, C. *Climate: A New Story.* Berkeley, California: North Atlantic Books (2018).

Eisenstein, C. 'From QAnon's Dark Mirror, Hope.' Charleseisenstein.org (December 2020).

Elwood, J., Andreotti, V., and Stein, S. *Towards Braiding.* Musagetes (2019).

Freud, S. *Civilization and its Discontents*. Translated by James Strachey. Penguin (2004).

Friedman, S. *The Glass Ceiling: Why It Pays To Be Privileged*. Policy Press (2019).

Furet, F. *The Passing of an Illusion: The Idea of Communism in the Twentieth Century*. Translated by Deborah Furet. University of Chicago Press (1999).

Gogol, N. V. *Revizor (The Government Inspector)*. Translated by William Harrison. Blackwell (1984).

Graeber, D. *Bullshit Jobs: A Theory*. Penguin (2018).

Graeber, D. *Debt: The First 5000 Years*. Melville House (2012).

Graeber, D. *The Utopia of Rules: On Technology, Stupidity, and the Joys of Bureaucracy*. Melville House (2016).

Gramsci, A. *Prison Notebooks*. Lawrence and Wishart (1973).

Gros, F. *A Philosophy of Walking*. Translated by John Howe. Verso (2014).

Hayek, F. von. *The Road to Serfdom*. Routledge & Kegan Paul (1962).

Hedges, C. *America: The Farewell Tour*. Simon & Schuster (2019).

Hedges, C., Sacco, J., and Peters, J. *Days of Destruction, Days of Revolt*. Bold Type Books (2014).

Hedges, C. *Death of the Liberal Class*. Nation Books (2010).

Herodotus. *The Histories*. Translated by Aubrey de Sélincourt. Penguin Classics (1999).

Herman, E. S., and Chomsky, N. *Manufacturing Consent: The Political Economy of Mass Media*. Pantheon Books (1988).

Herzen, A. *Letters from France and Italy (1847–1851)*.

Translated by Judith E. Zimmerman. University of Pittsburgh Press (1995).

Herzen, A. *My Past and Thoughts.* Translated by Constance Garnett. Chatto & Windus (1924).

Hine, D., and Kingsnorth, P. *Uncivilization: The Dark Mountain Manifesto.* Dark Mountain Project (2009).

Homer. *The Odyssey.* Translated by E. V. Rieu. Penguin Classics (2003).

Huntington, S. P. *Dead Souls: The Denationalization of the American Elite. The National Interest 75* (2004).

Illich, I. *Deschooling Society.* Penguin Education (1973).

Illich, I. *Tools for Conviviality.* Calder and Boyars (1973).

Irrigaray, L. *This Sex Which Is Not One.* Translated by Catherine Porter and Carolyn Burke. Cornell University Press (1985).

Jackson, W. *Becoming Native to this Place.* Counterpoint (1996).

Jackson, W. *Consulting the Genius of the Place: An Ecological Approach to a New Agriculture.* Counterpoint (2010).

Jackson, W. *Nature as Measure.* Counterpoint (2011).

Jain, M. *The Parrot's Training (Retold).* Banyan Tree (2016).

Jaspers, K. *The Origin and Goal of History.* Yale University Press (1968).

Jensen, R. *We Are All Apocalyptic Now: On the Responsibilities of Teaching, Preaching, Reporting, Writing, and Speaking Out.* Robert Jensen & MonkeyWrench Books (2013).

Jung, C. G. *Synchronicity: An Acausal Connecting Principle.* Translated by R. F. C Hull. Routledge & Kegan Paul (1972).

Jung, C. G. *Modern Man in Search of a Soul.* Translated by W. S. Dell. Martino Fine Books (2017).

Kapuściński, R. *Encountering the Other: The Challenge for the Twenty-First Century. New Perspectives Quarterly,* (June 2005).

Kapuściński, R. *Travels with Herodotus.* Translated by Klara Glowczewska. Albert A. Knopf (2007).

Karinthy, F. *Metropole (Epepe).* Translated by George Szirtes. Telegram (2008).

Kauffmann, S. *Reinventing the Sacred: A New View of Science, Reason and Religion.* Basic (2008).

Kierkegaard, S. *Fear and Trembling.* Translated by Edna H. Hong. Princeton University Press (1983).

Krall, L. *The Economic Legacy of the Holocene. The Ecological Citizen 2* (2018).

Kumar, S. *Earth Pilgrim.* Green Books (2009).

Kumar, S. *No Destination.* Green Books (1992).

Kundera, M. *Immortality.* Translated by Peter Kussi. Faber & Faber (1998).

Kundera, M. *The Unbearable Lightness of Being.* Translated by Michael Henry Heim. Harper Perennial (2009).

Kunstler, J. H. *The Long Emergency: Surviving the Converging Catastrophes of the Twenty-First Century.* Atlantic (2005).

Lançon, P. *Le Lambeau.* Gallimard (2018).

Latour, B. *Où Atterrir? Comment s'orienter en politique.* La Découverte (2017).

Lee, R. and Mason, A. *Population Aging and the Generational Economy: A Global Perspective.* Cheltenham (2011).

London, J. *The Call of the Wild.* Penguin Classics (2018).

Maimonides, M. *The Guide for the Perplexed*. Translated by
Michael Friedländer. Mineola, Dover Publications (1956).

Mann, T. *The Magic Mountain*. Translated by John E.
Woods. Vintage (1996).

Marcuse, H. *Eros and Civilisation*. Abacus (1972).

Marcuse, H. *One-Dimensional Man: Studies in the Ideology of
Advanced Industrial Society*. Routledge (1991).

Marquez, G. G. *Love in the Time of Cholera*. Spark
Publishing (2014).

McIntosh, A. *Riders on the Storm: The Climate Crisis and the
Survival of Being*. Birlinn (2020).

McIntosh, A. *Hell and High Water: Climate Change, Hope and
the Human Condition*. Birlinn (2008).

Meadows, D. H., Meadows, D. L., Randers, J. and W.
W. Behrens III. *The Limits to Growth*. Potomac
Associates (1972).

Meddeb, A. *Islam and Its Discontents*. Translated by
Pierre Joris and Ann Reid. William Heinemann
(2003).

Mitchell, T. *Colonising Egypt*. University of California
Press (1991).

Monbiot, G. *Out of the Wreckage*. Verso (2017).

Monbiot, G. *Heat*. Penguin (2007).

Montaigne, M. de. *The Journal of Montaigne's Travels in Italy:
In Italy by Way of Switzerland and Germany*. Translated
by William George Waters. BiblioLife (2009).

Morozov, E. *To Save Everything, Click Here: Technology,
Solutionism and the Urge to Fix Problems That Don't Exist*.
Allen Lane (2013).

Morozov, E. *The Net Delusion: How Not to Liberate the World*. Penguin (2011).

Murakami, H. *1Q84*. Translated by Jay Rubin and Philip Gabriel. Harvill Secker (2012).

Murakami, H. *Norwegian Wood*. Translated by Jay Rubin. Vintage (2001).

Murakami, H. *Kafka on the Shore*. Translated by Philip Gabriel. Alfred A. Knopf (2005).

Murakami, H. *The Wind-Up Bird Chronicle*. Translated by Jay Rubin. Vintage Digital (2011).

Nhất Hạnh, T. *Teachings on Love*. Element (2003).

Nietzsche, F. *Beyond Good and Evil*. Translated by R. J. Hollingdale. Penguin Classics (2003).

Nolte, E. *La Guerre Civile Européenne: National-Socialisme et Bolchevisme 1914–1945*. Perrin (2011).

Orwell, G. *Animal Farm*. Penguin (2008).

Panikkar, R. *The Rhythm of Being: The Gifford Lectures*. Orbis Books (2013).

Pauly, D. *Anecdotes and the Shifting Baseline Syndrome of Fisheries. Trends in Ecology and Evolution 10*. Cell Press (1995).

Piketty, T. *Capital and Ideology*. Translated by Arthur Goldhammer. Harvard University Press (2020).

Rabelais, F. *Gargantua and Pantagruel*. Translated by M. A. Screech. Penguin (2006).

Reiss, T. *The Orientalist: In Search of a Man Caught Between East and West*. Arrow (2006).

Renee Taylor, S. *The Body Is Not An Apology: The Power of Radical Self-Love*. Berrett-Koehler (2018).

Revel, J-F. *Les Plats de Saison: Journal de l'Année 2000.* Plon (2001).

Revel, J-F. *How Democracies Perish.* Translated by William Byron. Doubleday (1984).

Revel, J-F. *The Totalitarian Temptation.* Translated by David Hapgood. Secker & Warburg (1977).

Revel, J-F. *Histoire de la Philosophie Occidentale.* Agora (2003).

Rodney, W. *How Europe Underdeveloped Africa.* Howard University Press (1981).

Rischard, J. F. *High Noon: 20 Global Problems, 20 Years to Solve Them.* Perseus (2002).

Sacco, J. *Palestine.* Jonathan Cape (2003).

Saïd, E. *Orientalism.* Penguin (1985).

Saïd, E. *Out of Place: A Memoir.* Granta (1999).

Sarr, F. *Afrotopia.* Translated by Drew S. Burk. University of Minnesota Press (2020).

Sattouf, R. *The Arab of the Future: A Graphic Memoir.* Two Roads (2016).

Scott, J. C. *Against the Grain: A Deep History of the Earliest States.* Yale University Press (2017).

Seed, J., Macy, J., Fleming, P., and Naess, A. *Thinking Like A Mountain: Towards a Council of All Beings.* New Catalyst Books (2007).

Shaw, M. *Courting the Wild Twin.* Chelsea Green (2020).

Sheller, M. *Mobility Justice: The Politics of Movement in an Age of Extremes.* Verso (2018).

Singer, I. B. *The Magician of Lublin.* Translated by Elaine Gottlieb and Joseph Singer. Secker & Warburg (1961).

Stein, G. *The Autobiography of Alice B. Toklas.* Penguin (2001).

Stein, S., Hunt, D., Suša, R., and de Oliveira Andreotti, V. *The Educational Challenge of Unraveling the Fantasies of Ontological Security. Diaspora, Indigenous, and Minority Education 11.* Taylor & Francis (2017).

Tagore, R. *The Home and the World.* Translated by Surendranath Tagore. Penguin Classics (2005).

Thoreau, H. D. *Walking.* Tilbury House Publishers (2017).

Vargas Llosa, M. *Notes on the Death of Culture: Essays on Spectacle and Society.* Faber & Faber (2015).

Vargas Llosa, M. *The War of the End of the World.* Faber & Faber (2012).

Vitek, B. and Jackson, W. *The Virtues of Ignorance: Complexity, Sustainability, and the Limits of Knowledge.* University Press of Kentucky (2008).

Vitek, B. *God or Nature: Desire and the Quest for Unity. Minding Nature 4.* Center For Humans & Nature (2011).

Wells, S. *The Journey of Man: A Genetic Odyssey.* Penguin (2003).

Wells, S. *Pandora's Seed: The Unforeseen Cost of Civilization.* Random House (2013).

Wolf, E. *Europe and the People Without History.* Berkeley, California: University of California Press (2010).

Yunkaporta, T. *Sand Talk: How Indigenous Thinking Can Save the World.* HarperOne (2020).

Zizek, S. *Violence: Six Sideways Reflections.* Picador (2008).

Zizek, S. *A Left that Dares to Speak its Name: 34 Untimely Interventions.* Polity (2020).

Zizek, S. *Living in the End Times.* Verso (2011).

Zizek, S. *First as a Tragedy, Then as a Farce.* Verso (2009).

Zorn, F. *Mars*. Translated by Robert Kimer and Rita Kimer. Picador (1982).

Zweig, S. *The World of Yesterday*. Translated by Anthea Bell. Pushkin Press (2009).

NOTES

Introduction

1 As Donald Trump once described a number of sub-Saharan African countries in a meeting with lawmakers at the White House on 11 January 2018.
2 François Héran, lecture at the Collège de France (5 April 2018).
3 https://www.un.org/en/sections/issues-depth/migration/index.html
4 Goldin I., Cameron G., and Balarajan M., *Exceptional People: How Migration Shaped our World and Will Define our Future*. Princeton University Press (2011).
5 Shaw, M. *Courting the Wild Twin*. Chelsea Green Publishing Co. (2020).
6 Jackson, W. *Becoming Native to This Place*. Counterpoint (2016).
7 Sassen S. *Expulsions: Brutality and Complexity in the Global Economy*. Harvard University Press (2014), 149–151; Klein, N. *Let Them Drown – The Violence of Othering in a Warming World*. The Mosaic Rooms (4 May 2016) https://vimeo.com/166018049
8 Sheller, M. *Mobility Justice: The Politics of Movement in an Age of Extremes*. Verso Books (2018).
9 Kartha, S., Kemp-Benedict, E., Ghosh, E., Nazareth, A., and Gore, T. *The Carbon Inequality Era: An assessment of the global distribution of consumption emissions among individuals from 1990 to 2015 and beyond. Joint Research Report*. Stockholm Environment Institute and Oxfam International (2020).
10 Stein, S., Hunt, D., Suša R., and de Oliveira Andreotti, V. *The Educational Challenge of Unraveling the Fantasies of Ontological Security, Diaspora, Indigenous, and Minority Education*. Taylor and Francis (2017).

263

1. The Transformative Power of Migration

1 We named the think tank after Abd Al-Rahman al-Kawakibi, a leading nineteenth-century Syrian intellectual and reformist.
2 Fewer than 15 per cent of Muslims are Arab.
3 'Get out while you can, says Monsieur Scram', *The Times*, 1 July 2013.
4 Renamed the *International New York Times* in 2013 and the *New York Times International Edition* in 2016.
5 The tagline of the WEF.
6 Hedges, C., Sacco, J., and Peters, J. *Days of Destruction, Days of Revolt.* Bold Type Books (2014).
7 Eisenstein, C. 'From QAnon's Dark Mirror, Hope.' Charleseisenstein.org (December 2020).
8 Said, E. *Between Worlds. London Review of Books* (7 May 1998).
9 Goodhart, D. *The Road to Somewhere.* C. Hurst & Co. (2017).
10 Scred Connexion and Mafia K-1 Fry.

2. Going Places

1 Then the managing editor of the *International Herald Tribune* before becoming its executive editor and eventually the United Nations' under-secretary-general for global communications.
2 McIntosh, A. *Hell and High Water: Climate Change, Hope and the Human Condition.* Birlinn (2008).

3. Migration Goes Multilateral

1 The Kaufmann Reports via hbr.org/amp/2016/10/why-are-immigrants-more-entrepreneurial
2 https://news.gallup.com/poll/245255/750-million-worldwide-migrate.aspx
3 https://publications.iom.int/system/files/pdf/wmr_2020.pdf
4 https://www.nature.com/articles/s41562-017-0277-0#:~:text=Globally%2C%20we%20find%20that%20satiation,occurring%20later%20in%20wealthier%20regions
5 Pauly, D. *Anecdotes and the shifting baseline syndrome of fisheries. Trends in Ecology and Evolution 10*: 430. Cell Press (1995).
6 Clemens, M., and Postel, H. *Deterring emigration with foreign aid: An overview of evidence from low-income countries. Population and Development Review 44* (4): 667–693. Wiley-Blackwell (2018).

THE NEW NOMADS

4. The Power of Leaving

21 Dorling, D., and Tomlinson, S. *Rule Britannia: Brexit and the End of Empire*. Biteback (2019).
2 https://www.independent.co.uk/news/uk/politics/british-emigrants-europe-continental-brexit-deal-latest-leave-uk-a9166136.html
3 https://bibliothek.wzb.eu/pdf/2020/vi20-102.pdf
4 The eighteen-year-old, unarmed African American whose death after being shot by police in Fergusson, Missouri, led to prolonged unrest and the national recognition of the Black Lives Matter movement.
5 https://www.nytimes.com/2015/03/01/opinion/sunday/the-next-great-migration.html

5. Get Out!

1 'The Best Hope for France's Young? Get Out.' *New York Times* (29 June 2013).
2 See also Ronald Lee and Andrew Mason 'Population Aging and the Generational Economy – A Global Perspective'.
3 As in 'all about the Benjamins' – the face of Benjamin Franklin adorns American hundred-dollar bills; Mao Zedong's adorns hundred-yuan bank notes.
4 'India is not being overrun by immigrants.' *LiveMint* (18 July 2019)
5 https://www.theatlantic.com/business/archive/2012/10/think-were-the-most-entrepreneurial-country-in-the-world-not-so-fast/263102/

6. Refugees and Communities – '(Don't) Go Back To Where You Came From'

1 MacGregor, M., 'Spain's Canary Islands – still a magnet for migrants'. *Info Migrants* (11 June 2019).
2 Tomasello, M. *Why We Cooperate*. MIT (2009).
3 Monbiot, G. *Out of the Wreckage*. Verso (2017).

8. Rise and Fall of the 'Digital Nomad'

1 Huntington, S. P. *Dead Souls: The Denationalization of the American Elite*. The National Interest (2004)
2 https://www.washingtonpost.com/lifestyle/travel/with-the-pandemic-shutting-borders-digital-nomads-find-it-harder-to-roam/2020/05/14/5bb679d6-8f09-11ea-a9c0-73b93422d691_story.html

265

9. A Fire Brigade of Pyromaniacs

1 Friedman, S. *The Class Ceiling: Why it pays to be privileged.* Policy Press (2019).

2 Hickel, J., and Kallis G. 'Is Green Growth Possible?' *New Political Economy* 25: 4, 469–486, (2020). DOI: 10.1080/13563467.2019.1598964

3 Kuper, S. 'The Myth of Green Growth'. *Financial Times* (23 October 2019).

4 https://www.un.org/sustainabledevelopment/blog/2019/06/lets-talk-about-climate-migrants-not-climate-refugees/

5 The international climate science community is undertaking an extensive programme of numerical simulations of past and future climates. In the most pessimistic scenario (SSP5 8.5 – rapid economic growth driven by fossil fuels), the rise in mean global temperature is likely to reach six to seven degrees Celsius by 2100, which is one degree Celsius higher than in previous estimates.

6 Barfield Marks, S. 'Staying Grounded. *The Ecologist* (23 May 2019).

7 https://theicct.org/blog/staff/should-you-be-ashamed-flying-probably-not

8 Barfield Marks, S. 'Staying Grounded. *The Ecologist* (23 May 2019).

9 COP stands for Conference of Parties, the name of the conferences supposed to allow us to avert the ongoing climate breakdown, which have taken place each year since the 1990s, to little effect.

Conclusion

1 Shaw, M. *Courting the Wild Twin.* Chelsea Green Publishing Co. (2020).

INDEX

267

276